Magic Tricks Made Easy

Step By Step Instructions & Videos For Kids To Learn 54 Unbelievable Magic Tricks!

DARIEN CLEMONS

WiZO LEARNING

FREE BONUS

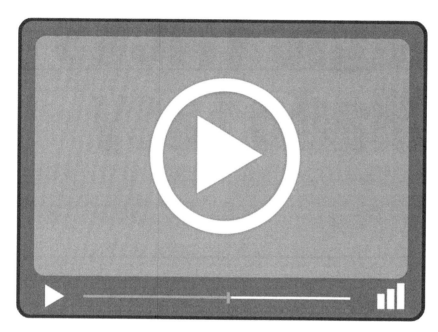

UNLOCK THE VIDEOS NOW!

Go To: ActivityWizo.com/magic

Please consider writing a review!
Just go to: activitywizo.com/review

ISBN: 978-1-951806-41-5

Table of Contents

What Can You Expect from This Book?

Welcome to our magic book! If you've decided to read this book, you are likely looking to learn a bit of magic and how to perform some tricks! You are in luck because not only will this book teach you how to perform nearly sixty different magic tricks, but you will learn how to make some of your props as well as the principles of magic, proper magic techniques, and the history of magic as an art form.

The magic tricks are laid out in three sections. Chapter One is the easiest set of tricks and will teach you many of the magic foundations needed to perform more complex magic. Chapter Two is full of fun magic tricks sure to impress your friends! Chapter Three are the most challenging tricks in the book but have no fear; once you master the basics, you will be ready to tackle these more complicated tricks. Chapter Four will give you an overview of the history of magic and additional resources to aid you in your quest to become a magician.

Why Learn Magic Tricks?

You may be wondering what the benefit there is to learning magic tricks? The good news is, there are many! One obvious benefit is that magic is fun! People of all ages, genders, and cultures love magic. It is fun to watch and perform!

Magic also helps you work on your hand-eye coordination. Most close-up magic uses techniques such as sleight of hand, misdirection, and palming. We will cover these more in-depth in a moment and go over them in some of the tricks themselves.

Much magic incorporates science. So as you go through this book and learn how to perform various tricks, you will learn some science too! The great part is that your audience will likely not know the scientific reasoning behind the trick so that it will seem like magic to them!

Magic gives you a chance to perform in front of others which is an excellent skill to have. Being able to get up in front of others to talk or perform is a skill that serves you throughout your entire life. It is important to be able to calm your nerves enough to stand up in front of others, whether it is to perform a show or simply present a school report. Mastering the ability to stand in front of others is a great confidence booster and will help with your communication skills. Learning to perform magic will help with your memorization and memory skills, as you will have to remember each step to perform each trick convincingly. The repeated practice builds self-discipline and increases your critical-thinking skills and problem-solving.

Magic inspires creativity and imagination. Once you learn how to perform the tricks in this book, performing magic will likely inspire you to try more daring and complicated ones, and you may even create some of your own!

Proper Techniques

When performing magic for an audience, you must be a performer! A magic show with no performance value will be dull and boring to watch. You will want to work on speaking with a clear and loud voice, smiling, and being charismatic. Your hands and gestures will play a significant role. It would help if you used them to draw attention to the right places at the right time, but be careful not to overuse them. It is a great idea to practice in front of a mirror or use a tablet or phone to record yourself. When you can watch yourself, you can see even the most minor things that may need improvement.

As you begin your performance, include an introduction to yourself and your show. After the introduction, it is a great idea to start with audience participation right away; this draws the audience and makes them invest in the show.

If a trick doesn't work correctly or falls flat, that's ok! Just move on. If a trick is messed up, acknowledge it, even laugh at yourself a little, but don't dwell on it. The audience is likely to be forgiving if you move on and wow them with the following trick!

Principles of Magic

According to Penn and Teller, two of the most famous magicians today, there are 7 Principles of Magic. They are: palm, ditch, steal, load, simulation, misdirection, switch, and lapping

Palm: To hold an object in an apparently empty hand
Ditch: To secretly dispose of an unneeded object
Steal: To secretly obtain a needed object
Load: To secretly move the needed object to where it is needed
Simulation: To give the impression that something hasn't happened yet
Misdirection: To lead attention away from a secret move
Switch: To secretly exchange one object for another
Lapping: To secretly slide an object into your lap.

At one point or another, you will use all of these techniques to perform magic. Some tricks will use several of these techniques all in one trick!

Chapter 1

Easy

Bend a Spoon Magic Trick

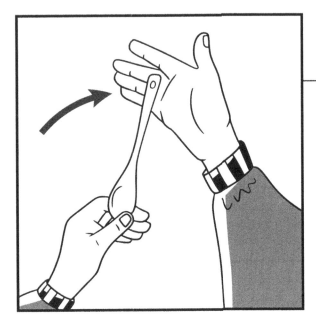

Step 1: Place the top of the spoon handle in the crevice where your fingers connect to the palm of your hand.

Step 2: Make a firm fist around the spoon and touch the rounded end to the table in front of you.

Step 3: Place your other hand over your fist.

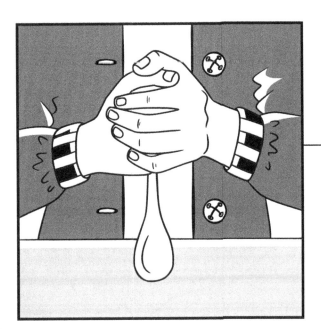

12

Step 4: With your second hand on top, slip the handle of the spoon between your pinky and ring finger without your audience seeing. This is called sleight of hand.

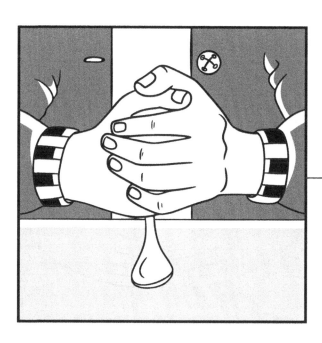

Step 5: From the front, it will still appear as if the spoon is in both fists. Make it look like it is hard as you bend your hand upwards.

Practice this trick in front of a mirror to be sure your second hand is covering the spoon handle as it falls backward.

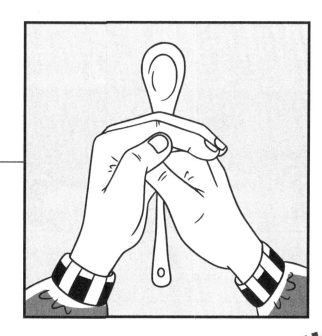

Disappearing Pencil

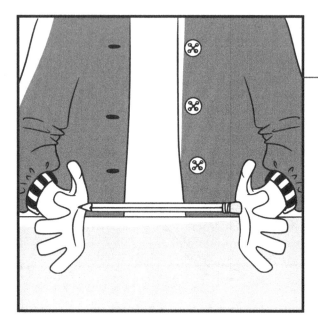

Step 1: Sit behind a table with a regular pencil. Place the point of each end in your palms.

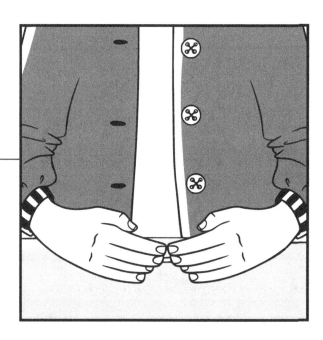

Step 2: Close your fingers in front of the pencil so that it is no longer visible to the audience.

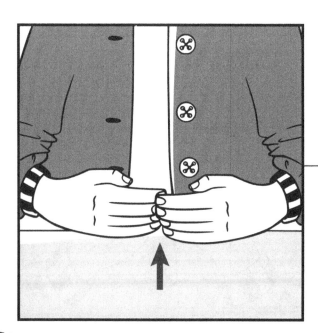

Step 3: Use misdirection by talking to your audience about the magic that will happen as you complete step 4.

Step 4: Slowly pull your hands towards the edge of the table and drop the pencil in your lap.

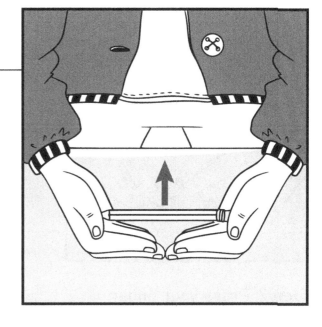

Step 5: Tell your audience to count to three with you.

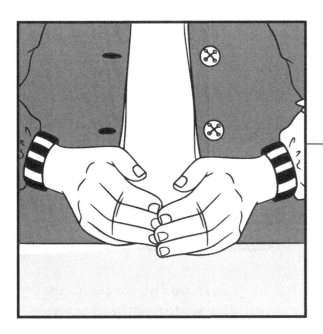

Step 6: On the count of three, clap your hands together to show you've made the pencil disappear.

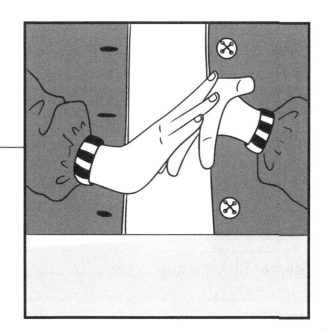

The Sugar Cube Magic

Step 1: Gather warm water, a sugar cube, a pencil, and a spoon.
Ask your friend to choose a number between 1–9. Write the number on the sugar cube, making sure it is dark.

Step 2: Press your finger firmly onto the number to transfer the graphite to your finger.

Step 3: Drop the sugar cube into the water without your audience seeing your finger.

Step 4: Stir the cup.

Step 5: Ask for the participant's hand.

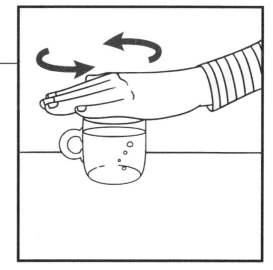

Step 6: Press the finger that touched the number into their palm as you guide their hand over the cup.

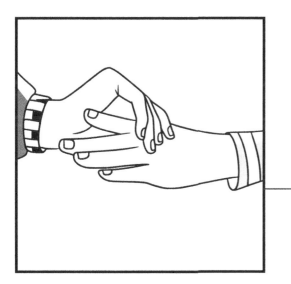

Step 7: Then, ask them to do a few magic swirls, palm down, over the cup.

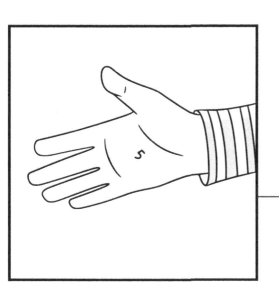

Step 8: Ask them to turn their hand over, and voila! The number should be on their hand.

The Color Changing Card

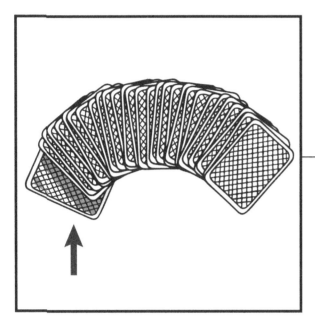

Step 1: Before performing, gather magician's wax and a double-sided card in two colors. Place a small piece of the magician's wax in the center of your double-sided card, on the side that is the same color as the rest of the deck. Place that card on the bottom of your deck with the opposite color facing up. Fan the deck out and ask someone to choose a card.

Step 2: Tell them to look at it, remember it, and place it on the bottom of the deck.

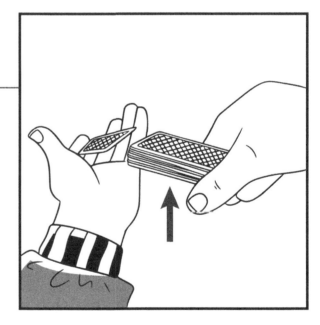

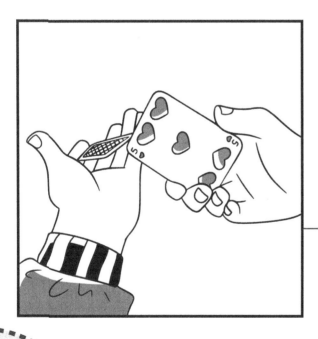

Step 3: Cut the deck in half a few times, and then for some flourish, you can tap it with a magic wand or wave your hands on top.

Step 5: Ask for the participant's hand.

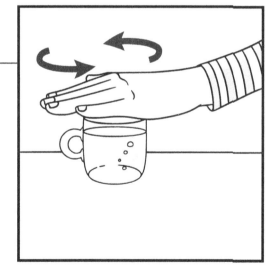

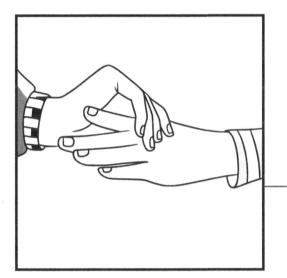

Step 6: Press the finger that touched the number into their palm as you guide their hand over the cup.

Step 7: Then, ask them to do a few magic swirls, palm down, over the cup.

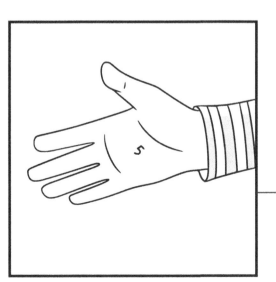

Step 8: Ask them to turn their hand over, and voila! The number should be on their hand.

The Rising Ring

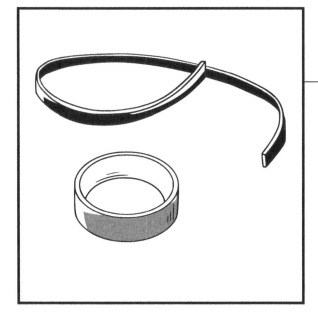

Step 1: Gather a cut rubber band and a ring. The ring needs to be evenly weighed for this trick to work.

Step 2: Place the ring on the rubber band.

Step 3: Pinch either side of the rubber band.

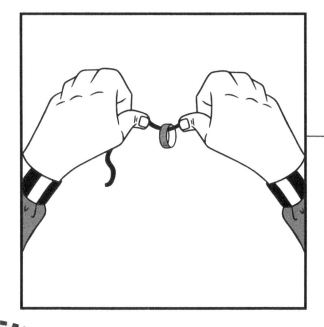

Step 4: Stretch one side up, pulling the rubber band very tight on the side being pulled up.

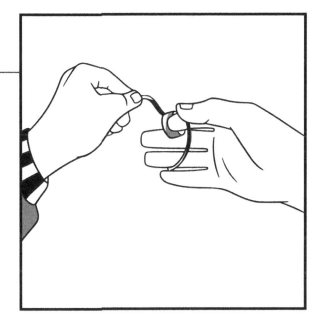

Step 5: Hold your hands so the ring is touching the thumb and index finger of the lower hand.

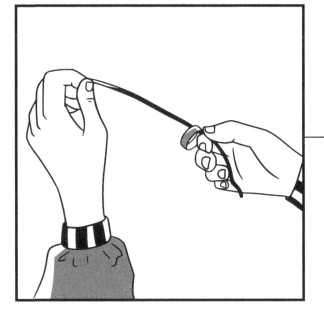

Step 6: Slowly release the tension from the rubber band from the lower hand as you pull upwards with the other hand. Let the rubber slide forward between your fingers slowly to prevent the audience from seeing the rubber band moving.

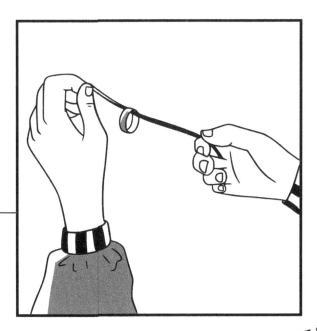

The Magnetic Hand

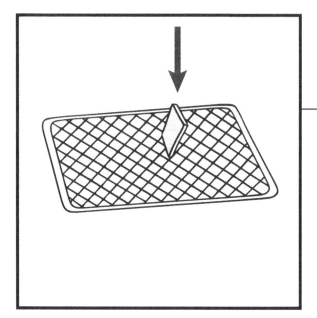

Step 1: Create a trick card by taking one card from your deck, cutting a tiny square flap from the back, and bending it. Glue the trick card to another card so that it looks like a regular card from the front.

Step 2: Even though the card is secure, keep your thumb over the card; otherwise, you'll give the trick away.

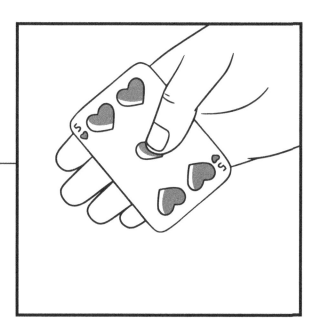

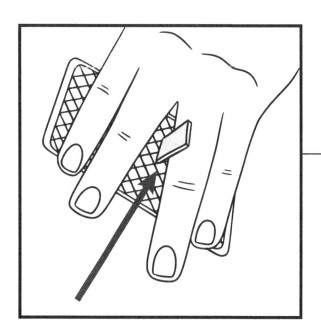

Step 3: Squeeze the tab on the trick card between your index and middle finger.

Step 4: With your palm face up and your thumb appearing to hold the magic card in place, slide four or five other cards under the trick card.

The pressure of holding your trick card in place will keep the other cards in place as you lift your thumb off.

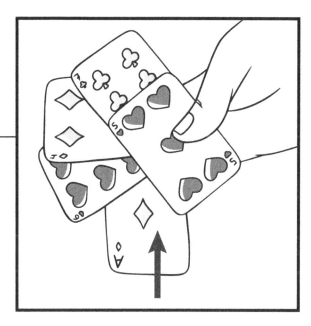

Step 5: To add some magic, you can tap your hand with a wand or wave your hand magically over the top.

Step 6: Release your thumb to make it appear as if it is floating.

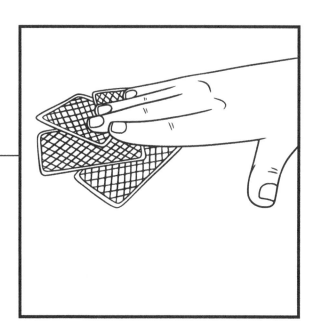

Jumping Paperclip

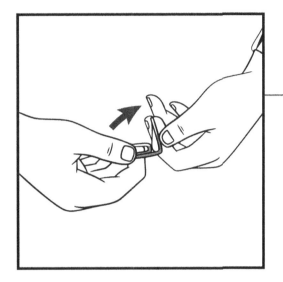

Step 1: The jumping paper clip may not be the trick that wows the audience, but it is a lot of fun to do! Grab a jumbo paperclip for this trick.

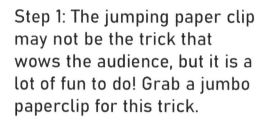

Step 2: Bend the large piece out.

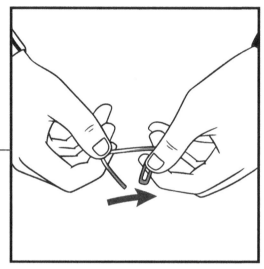

Step 3: Bend the smaller piece out to form a triangle.

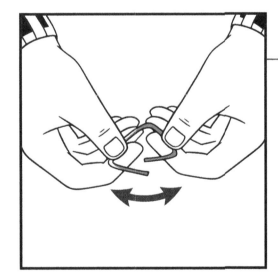

Step 4: Make the pieces as flat as possible.

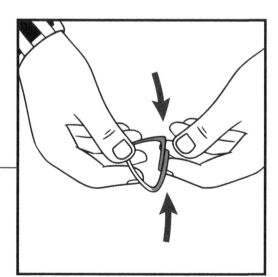

Step 5: Catch the two ends on each other.

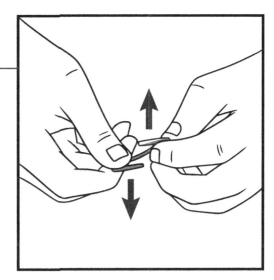

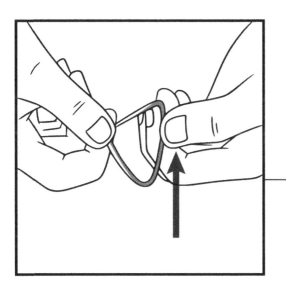

Step 6: You should have a triangle now.

Step 7: When you set it down, the paper clip ends pop open and appear to be jumping.

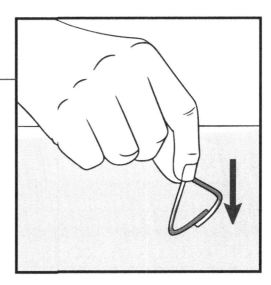

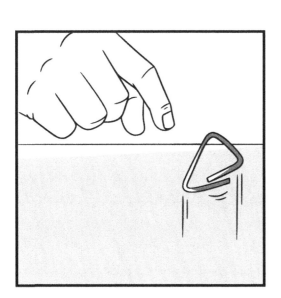

This trick may take some practice as well as some agility to get just right.

The Amazing Balancing Coin

Step 1: Gather two powerful magnets, a wooden ruler, two glass bottles, a quarter, a penny, and a paper to-go cup with a lid.

Step 2: Place the ruler on top of the two bottles like a bridge.

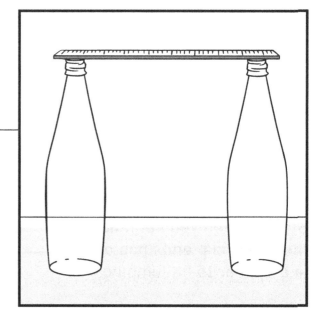

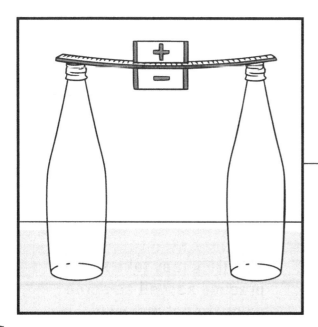

Step 3: Place one magnet on either side of the ruler, so they are hanging. The negative side of the magnet needs to be facing down.

Step 4: Place the cup underneath the magnets.

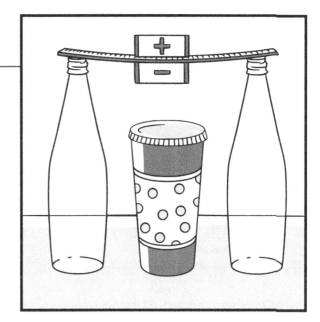

Step 5: Stack the coins. Put the penny on the bottom and the quarter on top.

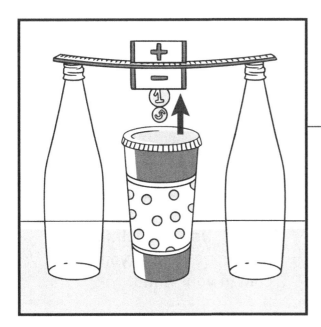

Step 6: The quarter should balance on top of the penny and look like it is floating.

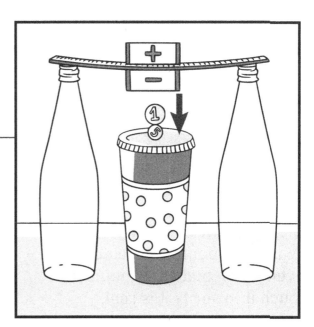

Bending a Coin

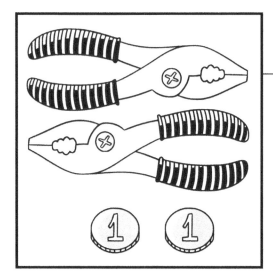

Step 1: You'll need two identical coins and two pairs of pliers.

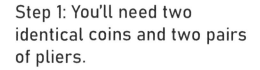
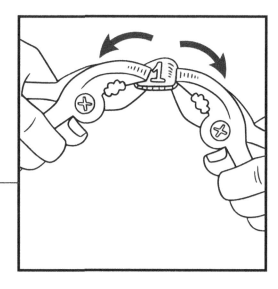

Step 2: Have an adult help you pre-bend one of the coins with the two pairs of pliers.

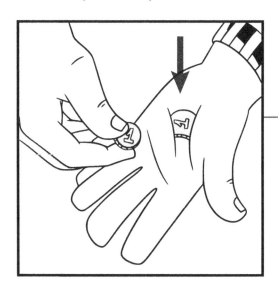

Step 3: Use the palming technique to hide your bent coin in your hand.

Step 4: Show the audience a regular, unbent coin. You can even let an audience member touch it to verify it is real.

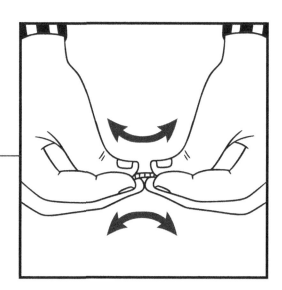

Step 5: Hold the coin in the same hand as your palmed one.

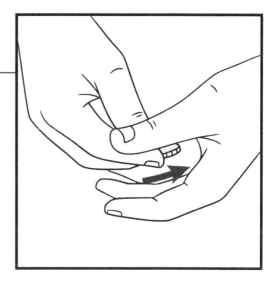

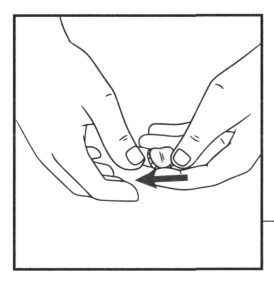

Step 6: Make a show of getting ready to toss the coin from one hand to the next but actually release the palmed coin into your other hand instead using the load technique.

Step 7: As you toss the palmed coin, roll the other coin down into your palm and hide it. This is the step you will need to practice over and over.

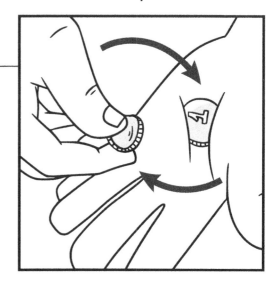

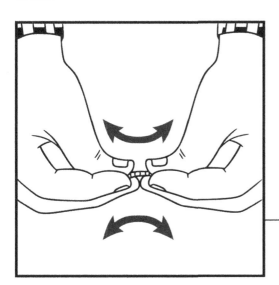

Step 8: Take the bent coin without letting your audience see that it is bent and pretend to bend it in front of the audience.

Eleven Fingers Trick

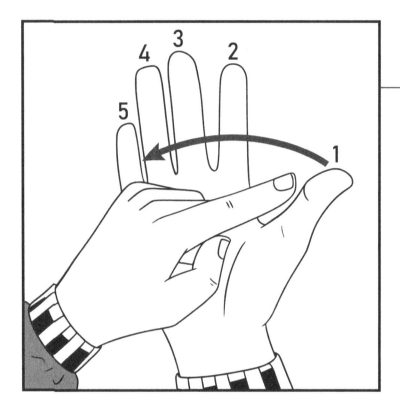

Step 1: Hold up your hands and start counting from one to ten.

Step 2: Once you've counted all ten fingers, say, "Hm, I thought I had 11 fingers!".

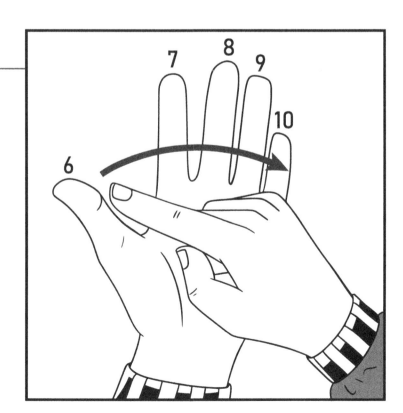

Step 3: Hold your hands back up and count backward from ten. "10, 9, 8, 7, 6".

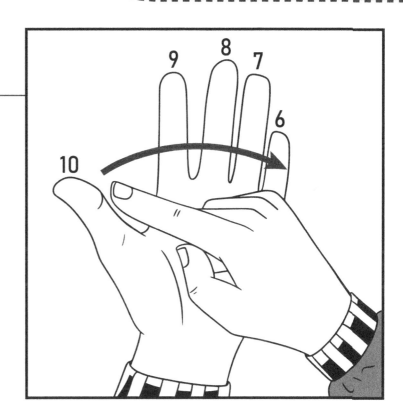

Step 4: Hold up your hand, show five fingers, and say, "See, six plus five equals 11!"

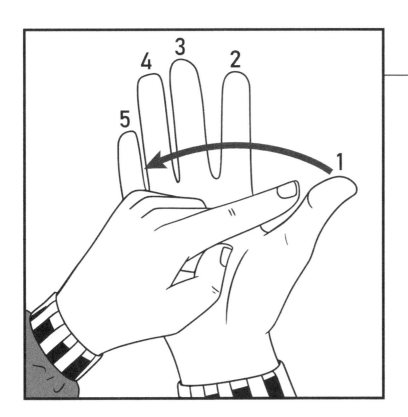

The Floating Egg

Step 1: Gather an egg, water, salt, and a large glass or vase to perform this trick.

Step 2: Before performing, pour a glass of water.

Step 3: Add roughly ½ c. of salt for one glass of water.

Step 4: Mix it well. ———

Step 5: Place the egg in the water and use the spoon to stir gently.

Step 6: If this is being performed as a magic trick, you can wave your hand or a wand to add to the performance.

Floating Needle Trick

Step 1: Gather a glass, a tissue, water, and a sewing needle for this fun magic trick!

Step 2: Fill a large glass with water to the point where the glass slightly overflows.

Step 3: Place a small piece of tissue on top of the water.

Step 4: Place the needle on top of the tissue and watch it float!

Step 5: Gently help the tissue to sink. But be careful not to touch the needle!

Step 6: The needle will float!

The Magical Moving Pencil

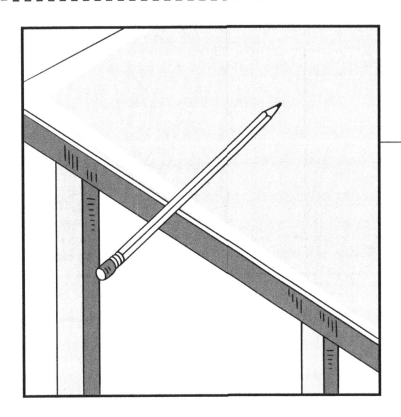

Step 1: This trick can be done anywhere you have a pencil and a table. Balance the pencil on the edge of the table as far as it will go without falling off.

Step 2: Use misdirection by adding some flourishes with your hands, and then place them down on either side of the pencil, leaving about six inches on either side.

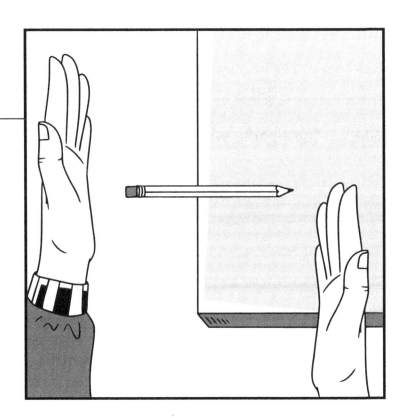

Step 3: Have the audience focus on your hands as you blow air out quietly to move the pencil. When done correctly, your misdirection will keep their eyes focused on the pencil.

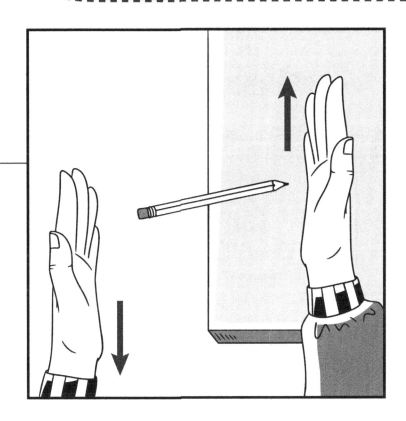

Step 4: As you blow air, move your hands so it looks like you are using magic to move the pencil.

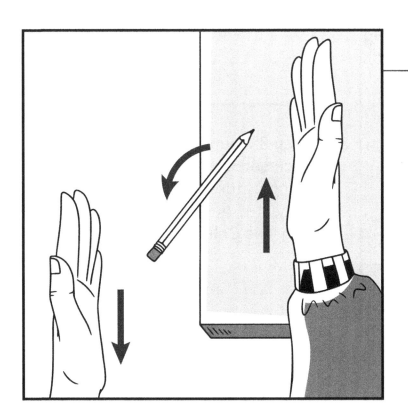

Instant Iced Trick

Step 1: Before performing this trick, gather a .5 liter bottle of water, a bucket of ice, a bowl, rock salt, and a thermometer

Step 2: Place a water bottle from the refrigerator into a covered large bowl of ice.

Step 3: Pour a generous amount of rock salt over the ice. Monitor the temperature. It must reach and stay at 17 degrees Fahrenheit (-8 degrees Celsius) for ten minutes.

Step 4: When it is ready and you are prepared to amaze your audience, very carefully take it out of the freezer. Make sure you DON'T shake it as you take it out.

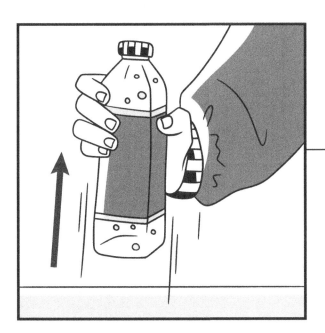

Step 5: To perform the magic, shake the bottle or bang it on the table.

Step 6: Watch as the entire thing freezes!

The Coin Pyramid

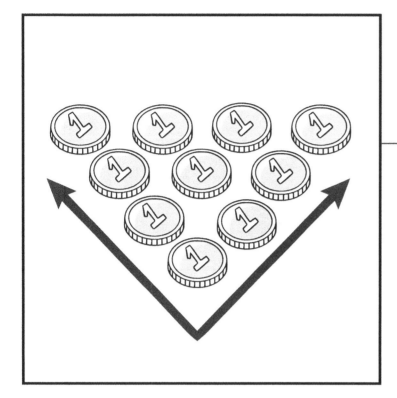

Step 1: Using ten coins of all the same type, make a pyramid with four coins at the bottom, then three, two, and one. Tell your audience you are going to flip the pyramid by only moving three coins.

Step 2: Slide the bottom two corners out and the top piece up to have a shape consisting of two coins, three coins, and two again.

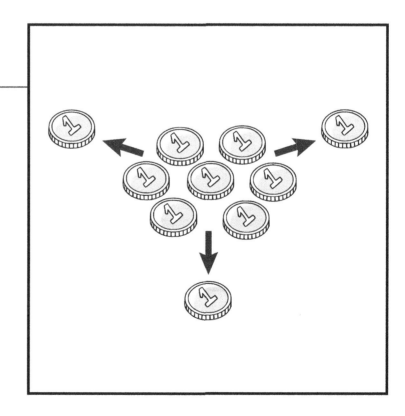

Step 3: Slide the bottom two pieces around to the other side and make that the new bottom.

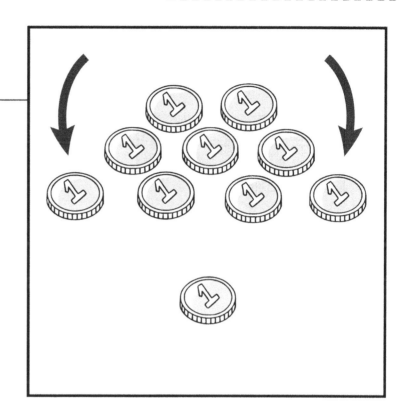

Step 4: Slide the original top coin all the way around to the other side and make it the new top of the pyramid.

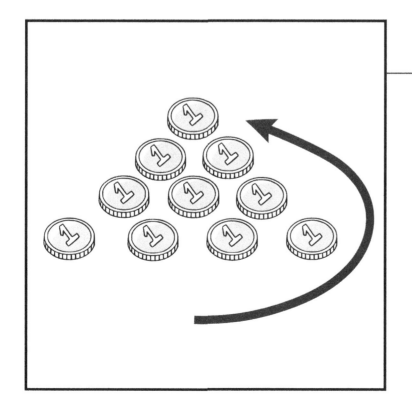

Magic Tube

Step 1: Decorate three cans with the following dimensions: 7 cm in diameter & 11 cm in height; 6.5 cm in diameter & 10 cm in height; and 5.5 cm in diameter & 8 cm in height. Remove the bottoms from the two larger cans.

Step 2: Fill the smallest tube with a long colorful ribbon that is attached to the bottom.

Step 3: Before performing, use hooks to stack the cans together and set them on the table

Step 4: Show the audience that the largest can is hollow before stacking it over the others.

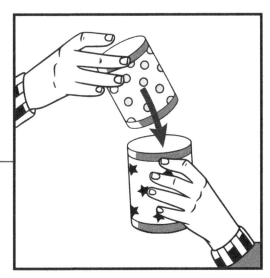

Step 5: Place the largest can over the medium one and pick them up.

Step 6: Allow the middle can to slide out and show the audience that it is also hollow. Then slide it back in.

Step 7: Use a magic wand, or wave magic hands over the can.

Step 8: Make it appear as if the ribbon came out of nowhere as you pull it out!

Unlinking Drinking Straws

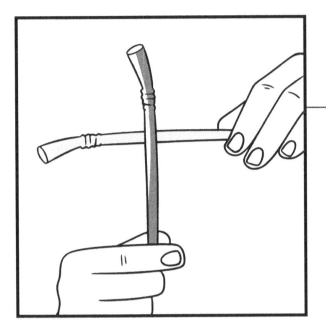

Step 1: Cross two different colored straws to make a T-shape. Straw A is verticle and in your right hand. Straw B is horizontal and in your left hand.

Step 2: Bend Straw A up and around Straw B from front to back.

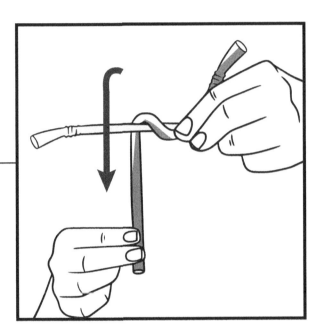

Step 3: Turn the straws once clockwise so that Straw B is now vertical.

Step 4: Wrap Straw B from front to back. It will look like the straws are knotted, but they will already be unknotted if done correctly.

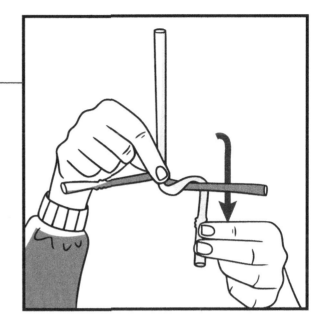

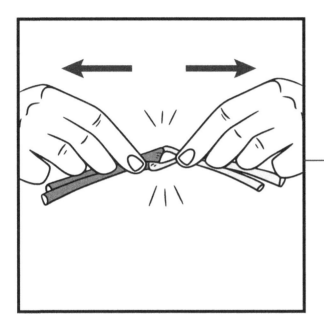

Step 5: Bend the ends of each of the straws together and hold them firmly between your thumb and forefingers.

Step 6: Say some magic words, then yank the pieces apart. It will appear as if you magically unlinked the straws!

Sliced Banana Trick

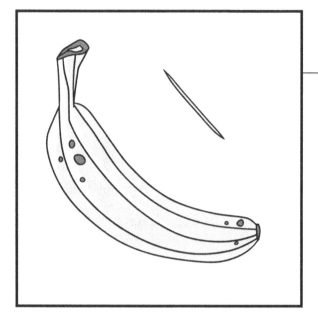

Step 1: Grab a banana and sewing needle. Find one of the banana's seams.

Step 2: Start at the top and insert the needle being careful not to go through the other side of the peel.

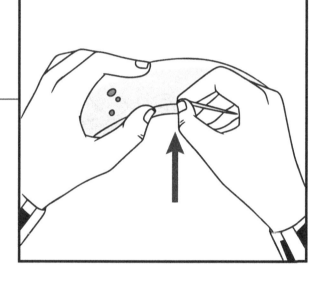

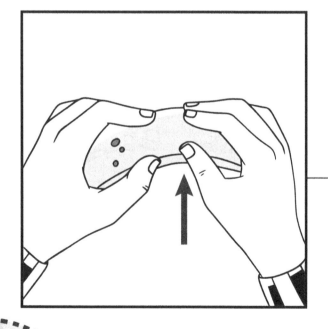

Step 3: Gently move the needle back and forth and up and down. This movement will slice the banana inside the peel. Insert the needle in as many spots as you'd like to slice the banana.

Step 4: Build a performance around the trick to entertain your audience and make it appear as if you're magically slicing it in the places cut with the needle.

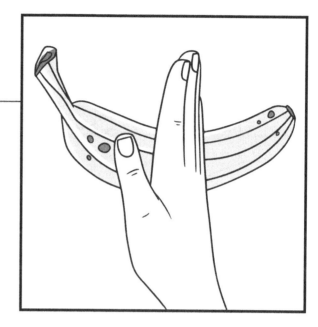

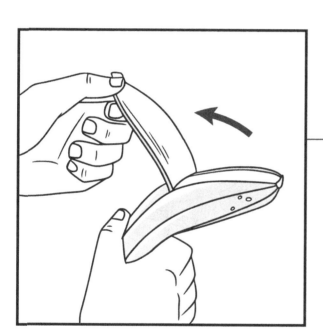

Step 5: Peel the banana.

Step 6: It should be sliced where you inserted the needle and pretended to chop.

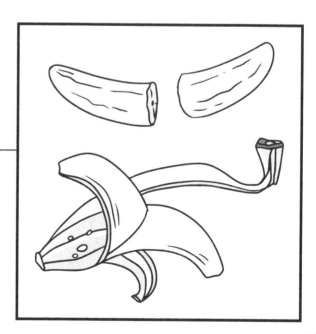

Straw Through a Potato

Step 1: Gather a pair of scissors, a straw, and a potato.

Step 2: Cut the drinking straw in half to make it easier to stab the potato.

Step 3: Cover one end of the straw with your thumb.

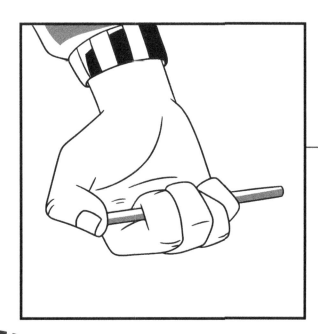

Step 4: Place the potato on the table in front of your audience.

Step 5: With one end covered, jam the straw into the potato.

Note: Add performance value by having an audience member try before or after you.

Chapter 2
Fun

Broken Matchstick

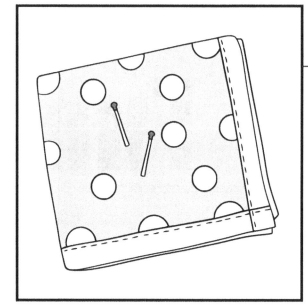

Step 1: Gather two matches and a handkerchief with an opening in the hem.

Step 2: Before performing, place a matchstick inside the hem of the handkerchief. When you are performing, show your audience how it is a regular handkerchief with nothing inside.

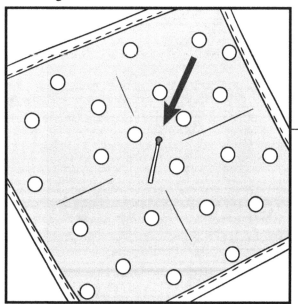

Step 3: Place the matchstick in the middle and fold the handkerchief.

Step 4: Hand the handkerchief to an audience member. Be sure to hand them the matchstick hidden in the seam.

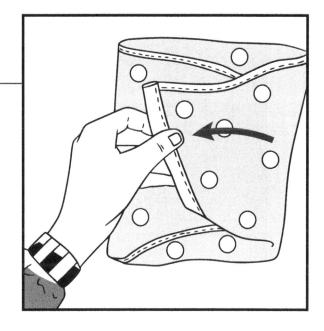

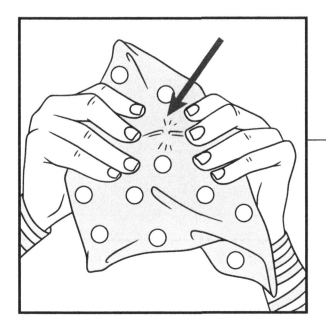

Step 5: Have them break the hidden matchstick.

Step 6: Take the handkerchief back from them, perform a little magic, then unfold the handkerchief to reveal that you have fixed the matchstick!

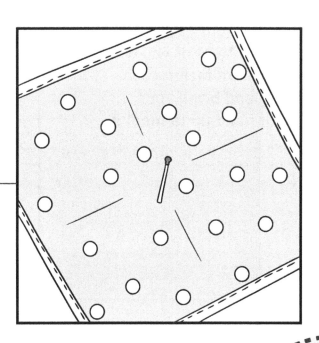

Pulling Thumb Away

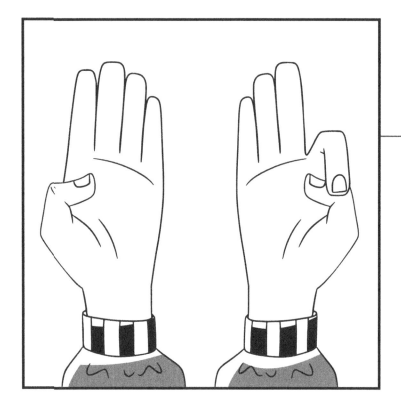

Step 1: Bend your left thumb down to the first joint. Bend your right thumb in a similar position and place your pointer finger over the joint on your right thumb.

Step 2: Hold your left hand in front of you with your palm facing your belly and bring your right hand up to meet it.

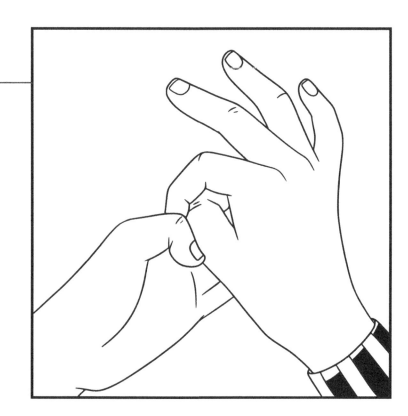

It should look like your thumb is attached and that you are holding it with your other hand.

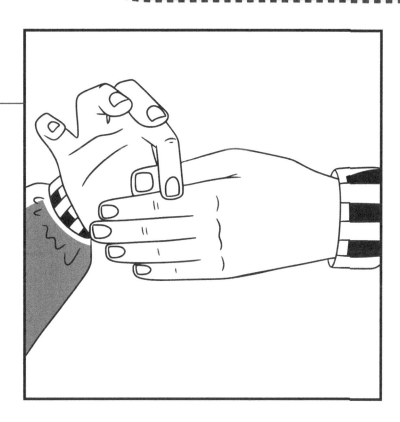

Step 3: When you are ready, pretend to pop your thumb off by sliding your right hand away.

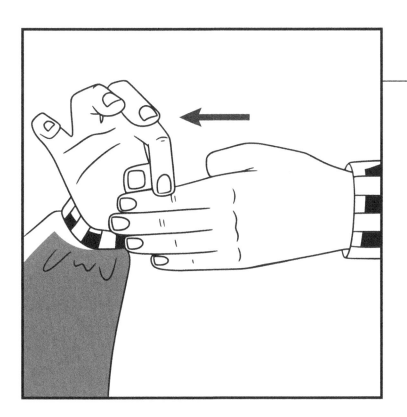

Finding a Spectator's Card

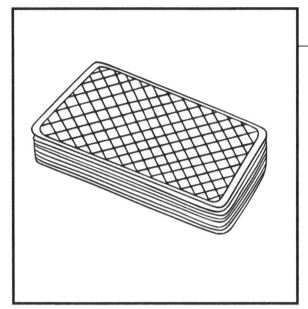

Step 1: Shuffle your deck of cards.

Step 2: Sneak a glance at the bottom card of the deck while shuffling.

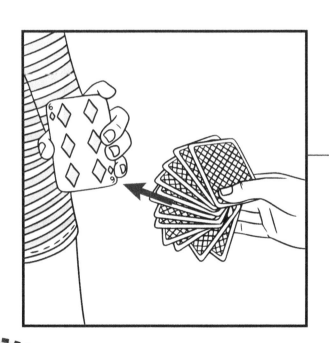

Step 3: Allow your spectator to select a card and remember it.

Step 4: Ask them to place their card on the bottom of the deck.

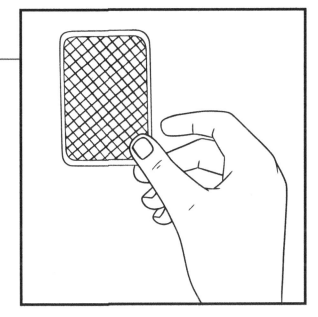

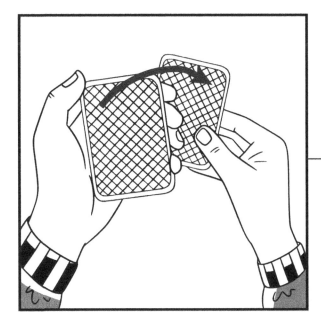

Step 5: Cut the deck a few times, making sure not to separate the bottom card you memorized and the spectator's card.

Step 6: Turn the deck over and fan them out. Wave your hand a bit for performance value, and then pull their card out! Their card is next to the card that was previously on the bottom of the deck.

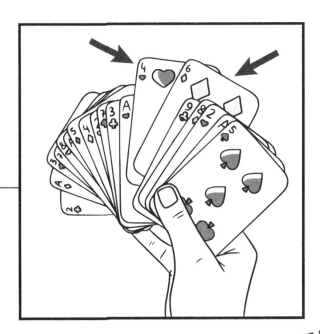

Rubber Pencil

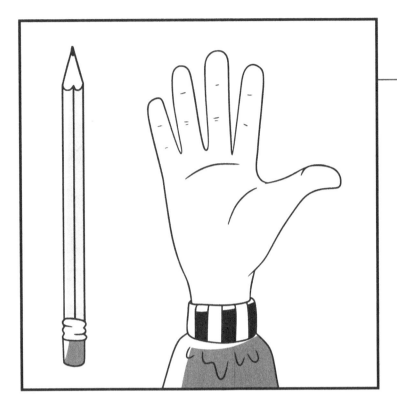

Step 1: All you need is a pencil and an audience member!

Step 2: Hold the pencil between your thumb and forefinger at the base of the pencil.

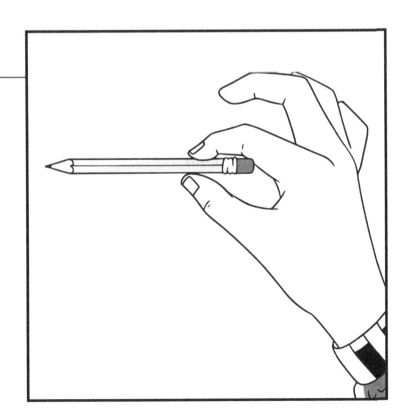

Step 3: Start waving your wrist up and down to make the pencil appear as if it's turned into rubber.

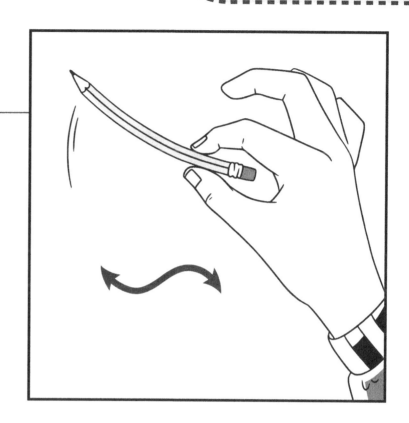

Tip: Do not squeeze the pencil too tight, or it will remain rigid.

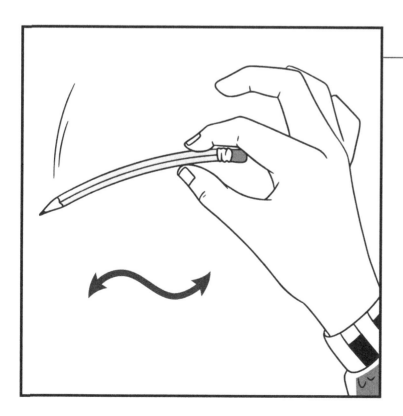

Talking Calculator Magic Trick

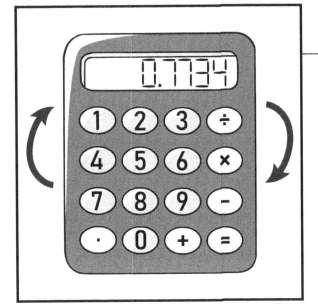

Step 1: Say hello to the calculator, then type in 07734.

Step 2: Turn the calculator upside down; it will read "hello."

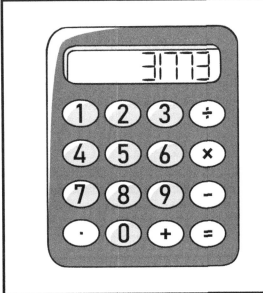

Step 3: Ask the calculator its name, then type in 31773.

Step 4: Turn the calculator upside down; it will read "Ellie."

Step 5: Ask the calculator its favorite place to go and type in 002.

Step 6: Turn the calculator upside down; it will say "zoo."

Magic Comb

Step 1: Rip the paper up into tiny pieces as you talk to the audience about your magic comb!

Step 2: Brush the comb through your hair as you say, "Not only is it magic, but it keeps me looking good too!"

Step 3: Say a couple of magic words, touch the comb to the paper.

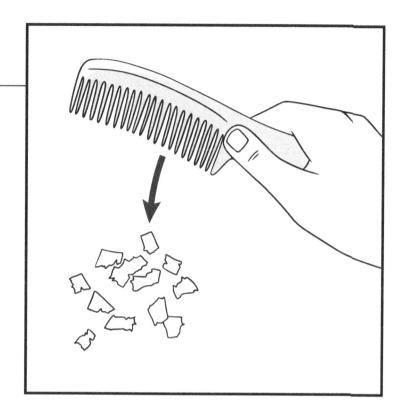

Step 4: Watch as static electricity magically attracts the paper to the comb.

Multiplying Coins

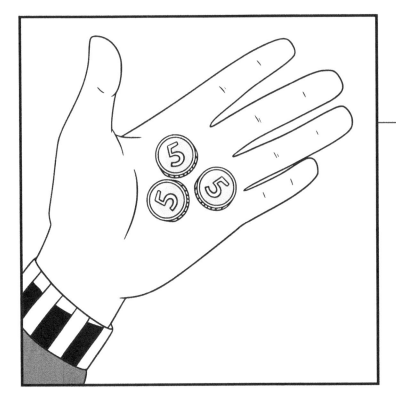

Step 1: Gather three of the same type of coin. They should look similar, meaning you shouldn't have two dull ones and one really shiny one.

Step 2: Palmone coin in your hand, hold up the other two coins and show the audience.

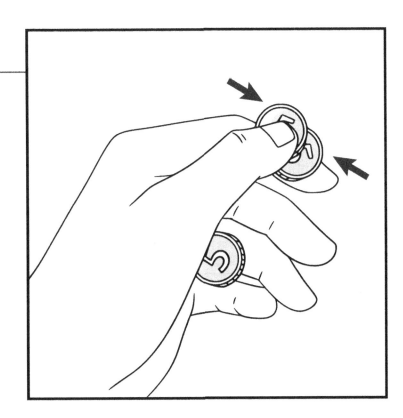

Step 3: Rub the coins together as you say your magic words of choice and close them in your palm.

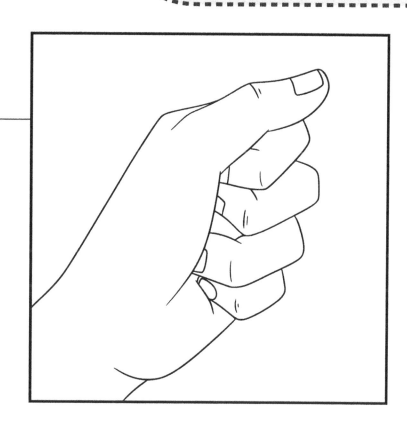

Step 4: Open your hand and show the audience that you have three coins now!

Floating Ketchup Trick

Step 1: Gather a tall, clear plastic bottle filled with water and a ketchup packet.

Step 2: Place the ketchup packet into the plastic bottle and screw the lid on tightly.

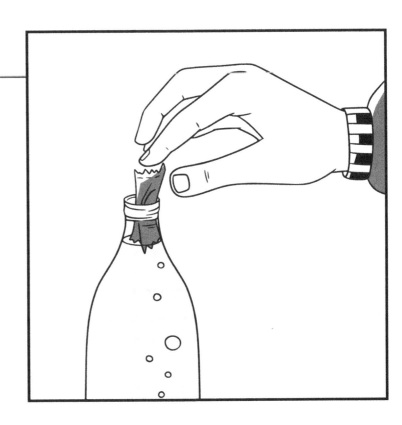

Step 3: Pretend to focus on the ketchup packet as you place your hand around the bottle. When you want the ketchup to sink, gently squeeze the bottle, and release the pressure for the ketchup to rise.

Tip: When you squeeze, be very subtle so that your audience cannot tell you are applying or releasing pressure. Use your other hand to make it look like you are making the ketchup rise and fall.

Pepper and Water Magic Trick

Step 1: Gather a plate, dish soap, water, and black pepper to perform this unique magic trick.

Step 2: Pour a layer of water onto the plate and sprinkle pepper onto the plate.

Pepper and Water Magic Trick

Step 3: Dab dish soap onto your finger.

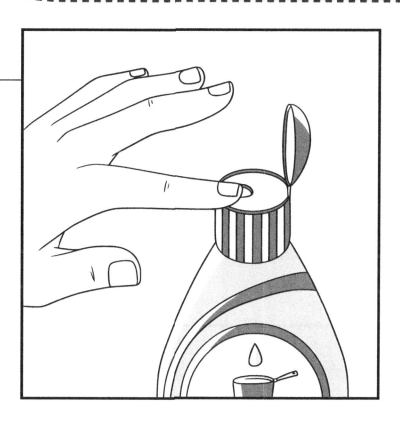

Step 4: Gently touch the center of the water. As you touch the dish soap to the water and pepper mixture, the pepper will scatter out to the edges of the plate.

Step 1: Gather a washable black marker, a pin, and a place to drain the soda like a bowl or the sink.

Step 2: Use the pin to poke a small hole in the can in a place where it won't be noticeable.

Step 3: Drain about a third of the soda in the sink.

Step 4: Color the opening portion of the can black so it looks like it is open.

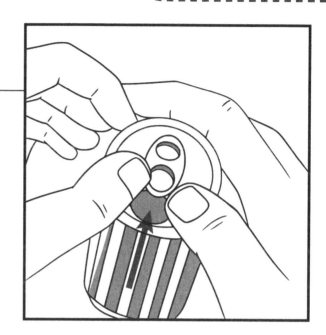

Step 5: Present the can to the audience with your thumb over the hole. Hold the can as if you are going to dump it out. After the audience is convinced, the can is empty, slightly crush it.

Step 6: Gently shake the can, and it will expand to its original shape. Once it is reformed, discretely rub off the marker to show it is magically whole again. Open the can and pour out the soda.

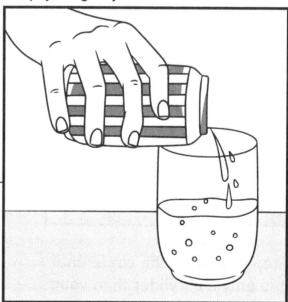

Silk Through Rope

Step 1: Gather two feet of rope and a silky hanky to perform this trick.

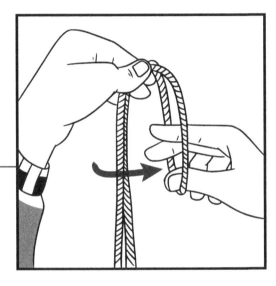

Step 2: Fold the rope in half to form a loop.

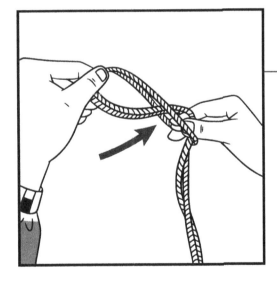

Step 3: Reach through the loop and pull the ends through, making a circle.

Step 4: Tighten the circle until it is only a bit wider than your fingers.

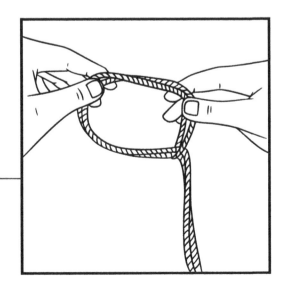

Step 5: Thread the hanky through the opening you made in the rope and pull the rope tighter.

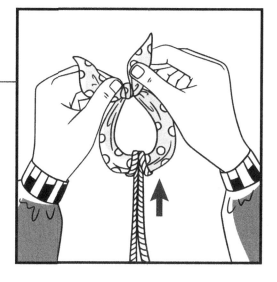

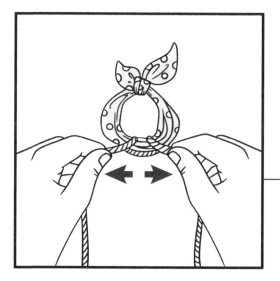

Step 6: Pull the ends of the hanky up and tie them together.

Step 7: Grab the two pieces of rope, one in each hand, and pull them away from each other.

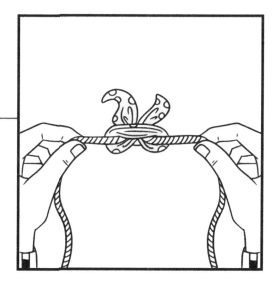

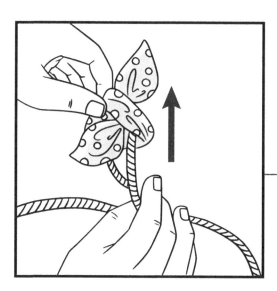

Step 8: Lastly, grab the hanky and tug at it, and viola, the hanky appears to have magically gone through the rope!

The Linking Paper Clips

This fun trick is easily done with two paper clips and a dollar bill.

Step 1: Fold a dollar bill in thirds.

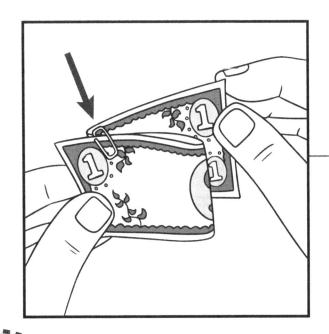

Step 2: Place one paper clip on the left corner connecting the front and middle piece.

Step 3: Place the second one on the right corner on the middle and back fold.

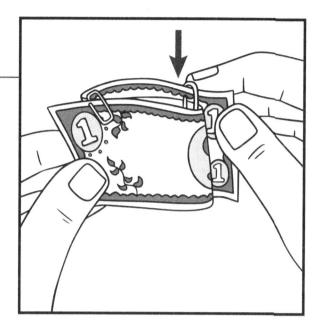

Step 4: Slowly pull the ends of the dollar bill away from each other.

As you pull, the paper clips will magically link together and jump off the dollar bill.

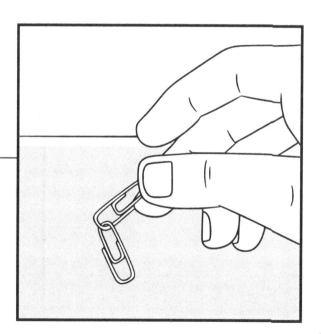

Walk Through Paper Trick

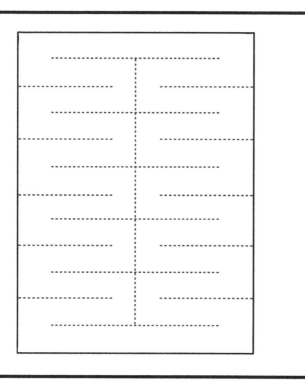

Step 1: This a fun little trick that will test your cutting skills! Gather a piece of construction paper, a pencil, a template from online of this trick, and a pair of scissors.

Step 2: Start the trick by telling the audience you are going to walk through a piece of paper!
Draw a sample template on your piece of paper and fold the paper in half lengthwise.

Step 3: Cut a piece of paper with a template along the dotted lines.

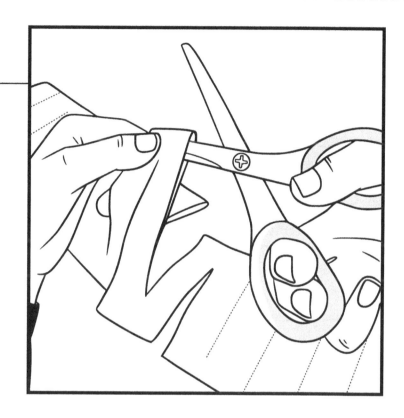

Step 4: Stretch the paper apart carefully and walk through it. It would be best if you practiced this enough times so that you have the cuts memorized. Cutting the paper more naturally as you talk to the audience will make the trick run smoother and increase the performance value.

Mind Reading Trick with Numbers

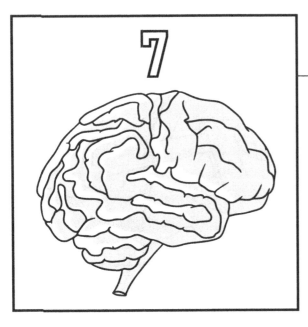

Step 1: Tell your audience participant to choose any number between one and ten.

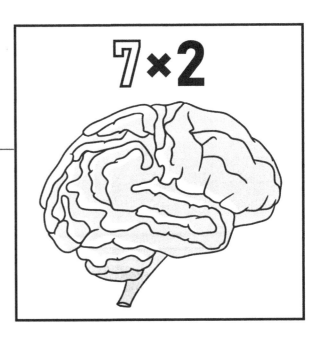

Step 2: Tell your participant to multiply their number by 2.

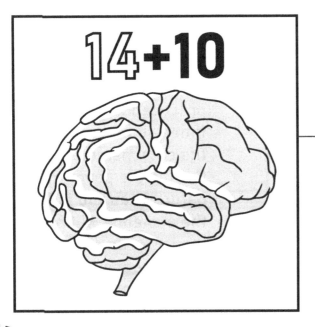

Step 3: Ask them to add 10 to their total.

Step 4: Next, ask them to divide their total by 2.

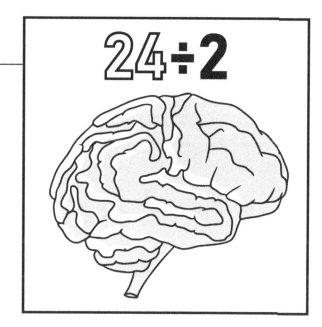

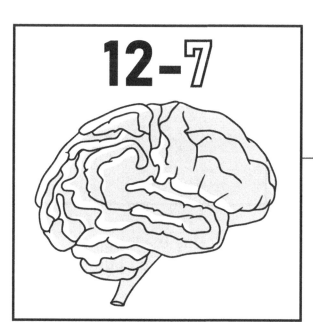

Step 5: Last, ask them to subtract their current total from their original number.

Step 6: Tell them the new number in their head is 5! The trick is when you asked them to add 10. No matter what the original number is, if you ask them to add 10 in this step, the answer will always be 5.

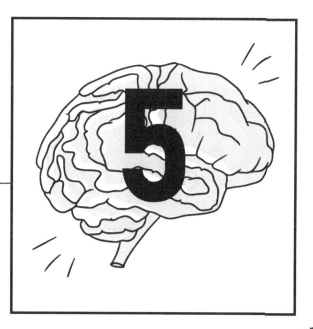

Pass a Coin Through a Table

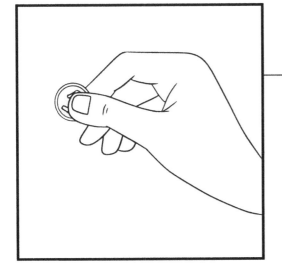

Step 1: Hold a coin in your hand, show it to your audience so they can see it is a real coin.

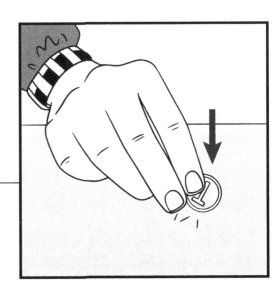

Step 2: Bang it on the table to show it is real.

Step 3: Use the lapping technique as you pull the coin towards you.

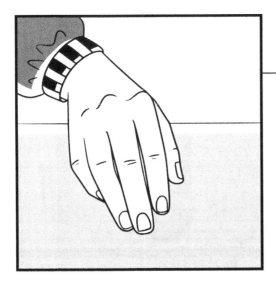

Step 4: Pretend to pick it up while you actually drop it in your lap.

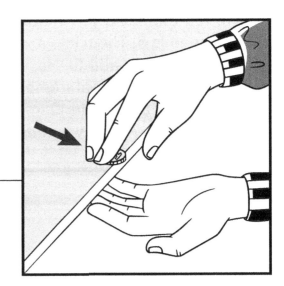

Step 5: Once the coin is in your lap, secretly pick it up with your other hand. Keep the hand you originally had the coin pinched as if you were still holding it.

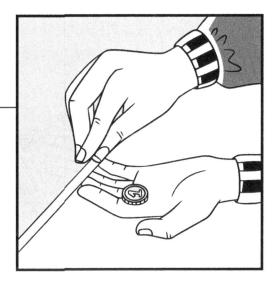

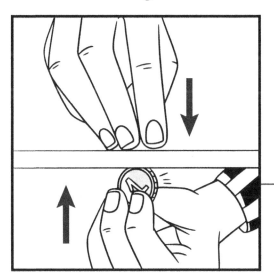

Step 6: Pretend to bang the coin on the table while at the same time you are actually banging the coin from underneath the table. You're creating the auditory illusion that you are still holding the coin in the original hand.

Step 7: Then pretend to flatten your hand into the table, which makes the coin disappear.

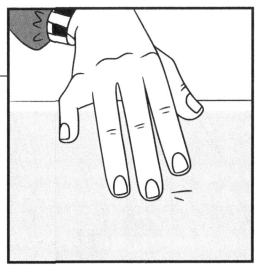

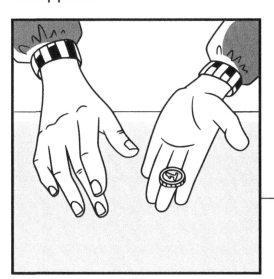

Step 8: Slowly bring the other hand up and show that the coin magically went through the table.

The Rising Card

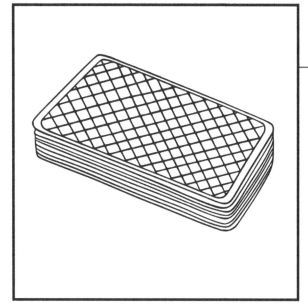

This trick is sure to wow your audience, and the best part is it is so simple and fun to perform!

Step 1: Allow your spectator to pick any card they would like from the deck.

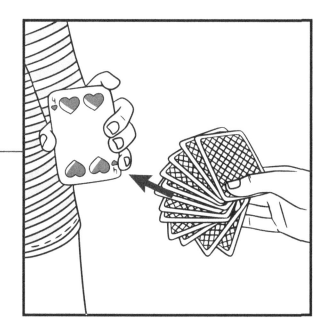

Step 2: Tell them that they need to remember their card.

Step 4: Stretch one side up, pulling the rubber band very tight on the side being pulled up.

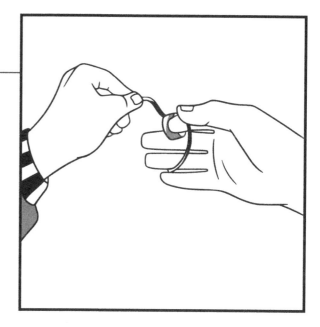

Step 5: Hold your hands so the ring is touching the thumb and index finger of the lower hand.

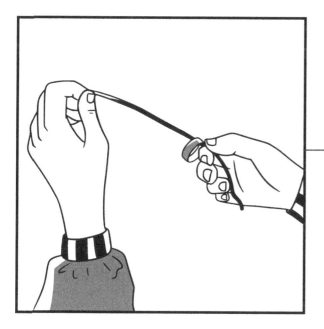

Step 6: Slowly release the tension from the rubber band from the lower hand as you pull upwards with the other hand. Let the rubber slide forward between your fingers slowly to prevent the audience from seeing the rubber band moving.

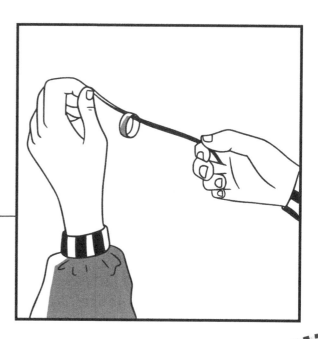

Cut and Restored Baloon Trick

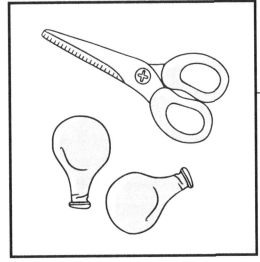

Step 1: The cut and restore balloon trick is a fun party trick that you can perform anytime you have two balloons of the same color and a pair of scissors!

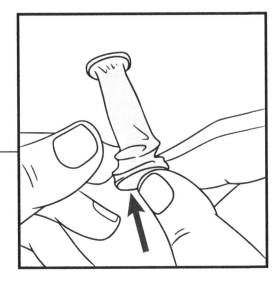

Step 2: Take a balloon and tuck it inside itself from the closed-end as if you were rolling a pair of socks up.

Step 3: Cut the mouth of the other balloon.

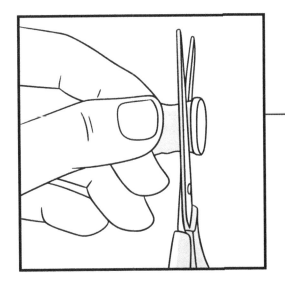

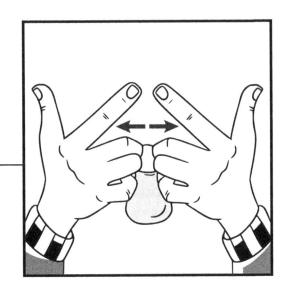

Step 4: Stretch the balloon but leave your thumbs and index fingers free for convenience.

Step 5: Place the tucked-up balloon inside.

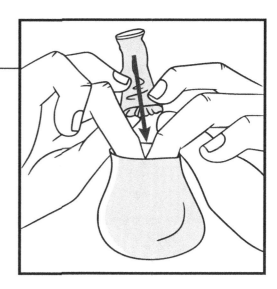

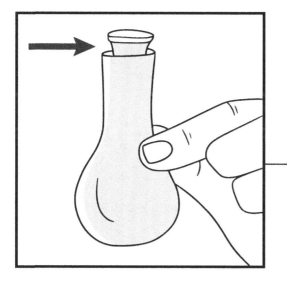

It should now look like you have one balloon.

Step 6: Cut the bottom of the balloon off and then perform whatever magic you want to make it seem as if you're restoring the balloon.

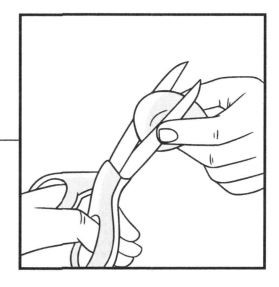

Step 7: When ready, blow air into it, and the tucked-up balloon should pop out and blow up, making it look as if you've magically repaired the balloon.

Chapter 3
Challenging

Hovercard Magic

Step 1: Gather a deck of cards, clear tape, and scissors.

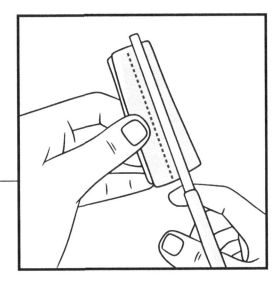

Step 2: Fold a card in half and cut two thin strips off the outer edge of the card.

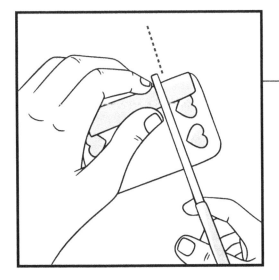

Step 3: Cut the first quarter of those first two strips off. You should now have two long strips and two short pieces.

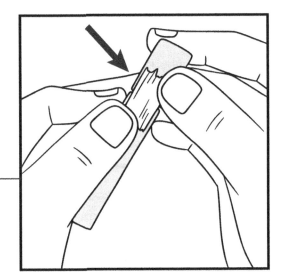

Step 4: Join the four pieces together to make a rectangular frame.

Step 5: The frame needs to be flexible so that it can fold flat.

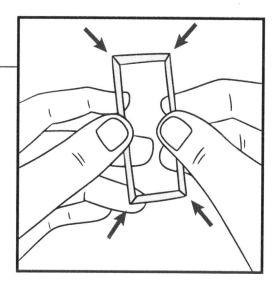

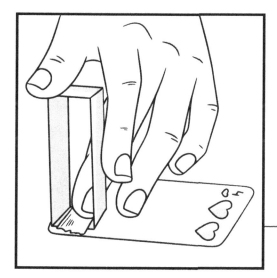

Step 6: Tape the flattened frame to the joker or extra card in the deck at one end. Once taped, this piece should fold up and down like a lever.

Step 7: Extend the frame and use a clear piece of tape to attach the card that will hover or float. You should now be able to fold and unfold the piece, making it appear as if the card is levitating.

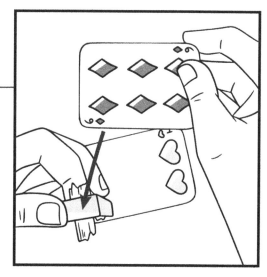

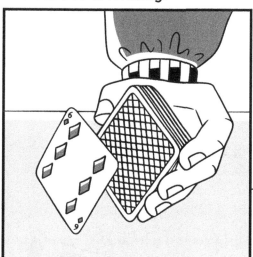

Tip: Practice this trick in front of the mirror or record yourself to make sure you can perform the trick while concealing the secret piece taped inside.

Impossible Egg Crush

Step 1: Practice this trick over the sink before performing; that way, if it doesn't work the first few times, you don't have as big of a mess to clean up.

Step2: Start by crushing an egg or having an audience member crush or hold an egg to prove it is real. Warning: this is messy but will show off you are using real eggs.

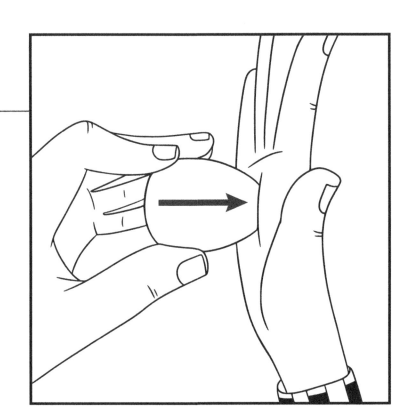

Step 3: Wave a magic wand or recite some magic words to make the egg unbreakable for audience effect.

Step 4: Place the base of the egg in your palm and press on both ends of the egg with equal pressure with both hands.

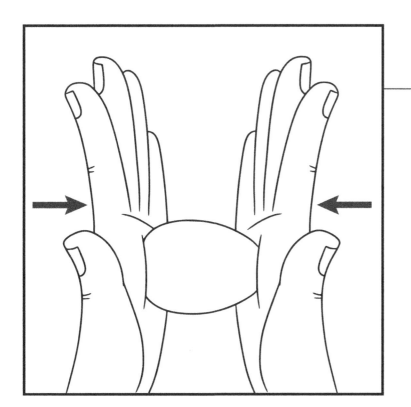

Stunning Coin Through Glass Magic Trick

Step 1: Allow your spectator to examine the coin and the glass to prove that they are real.

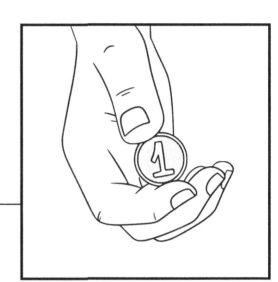

Step 2: As you take the coin back, use the load technique to make it look as if you dropped it into your lower palm.

Step 3: Do this by tilting your top hand and quickly closing your bottom palm.

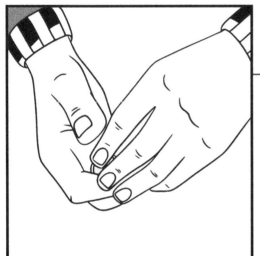

When done correctly, the coin is hidden in the top hand, which is how you will drop it into the glass.

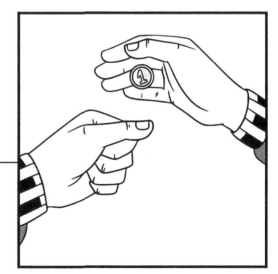

Stunning Coin Through Glass Magic Trick

Step 4: Keep the coin hidden between your fingers.

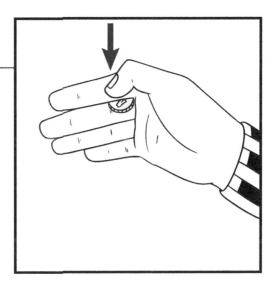

Step 5: Pick up the glass using the hand with the hidden coin while your opposite palm remains closed.

Step 6: Keep your palm closed as you tap it a few times against the bottom of the glass.

Step 7: When you are ready, the last time you hit the bottom of the glass, release the coin from your top hand into the glass.

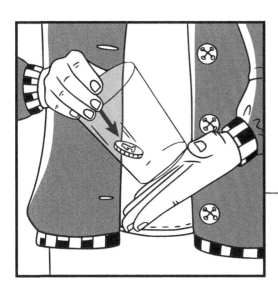

Disappearing Water

To perform this trick, you need three solid cups you can't see through and some sodium polyacrylate.

Step 1: Before performing, add about 1 tablespoon of sodium polyacrylate to one of the cups. You may need to experiment a bit to test the right amount.

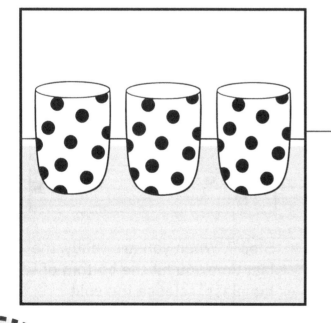

Step 2: Gather your audience and place the three cups in a row.

Step 3: Add ¼ cup of water to the cup with the sodium polyacrylate.

Step 4: Switch and slide the cups around several times as you talk to the audience; then until the water has turned to a gel.

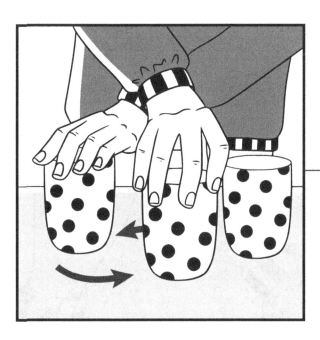

Step 5: Stop switching the cups around and flip the cups upside down. Since no water has come up, the audience will believe you've made it disappear!

Cut A Pencil In Half

Step 1: Before performing, ask an adult to help you cut the pencil almost all the way through.

Step 2: Fold the dollar bill or paper in half lengthwise.

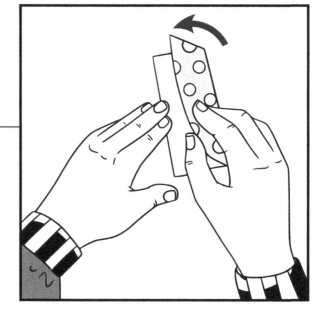

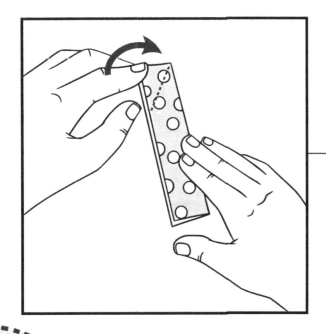

Step 3: Fold back one of the corners. The idea is to make it look like a knife.

Step 4: Place the pencil against the edge of the table.

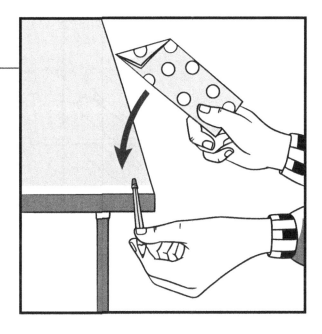

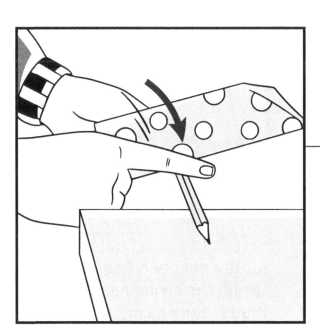

Step 5: Hide your index finger behind the paper.

Step 6: As you bring the paper down using your finger to apply force causing the pencil to break the rest of the way.

String Figure Magic Trick

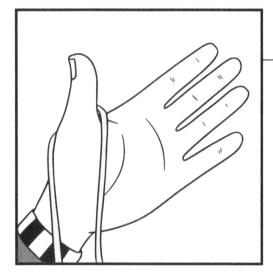

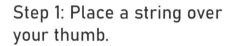
Step 1: Place a string over your thumb.

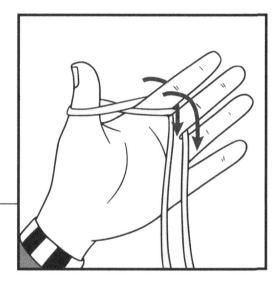

Step 2: Take the string that is on the outside of your thumb and wrap it behind the next finger. Take the string nearest your thumb and wrap it around your middle finger.

Step 3: Continue that pattern for the next two fingers, taking the string nearest your thumb and placing it behind the next finger.

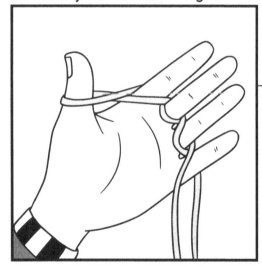

Step 4: Take the piece of string on the outside of your pinky and bring it across your palm and let it rest there.

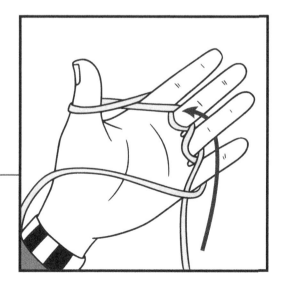

Step 5: Take the other string (not on your palm) and wrap it behind your ring finger.

Step 6: Take the string closest your pinky and put it over your middle finger. Continue that pattern by taking the string closest to the pinky and wrapping it behind the next finger.

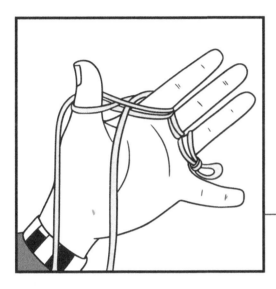

Step 7: This pattern, when completed, looks very complicated, but all you need to do next is to move your pinky from the string loop.

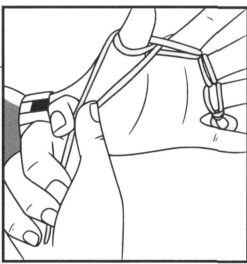

Step 8: Grab both pieces of string and give it a tug. It will magically unlink the entire string!

The Crayon Magic

Everyone loves a trick that seems like it uses some mind-reading! You can use any set of four or five crayons.

Step 1: Hold the crayons behind your back.

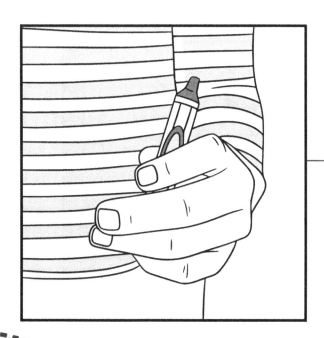

Step 2: Tell your audience participant to choose the crayon of their choice.

Step 3: Have them place the crayon of choice back into your empty hand.

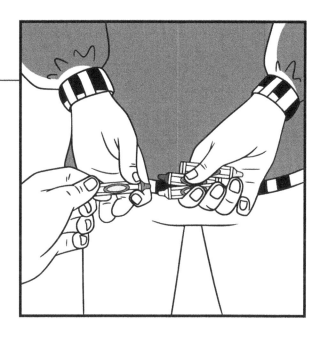

Step 4: Once the crayon is back in your hand, turn around and secretly use the crayon to color your nail.

Step 5: When you turn to face your audience, mix all the crayons together and sneak a glance at your nail, making sure to conceal the color. After a magic wave or two, select the crayon you colored on your nail!

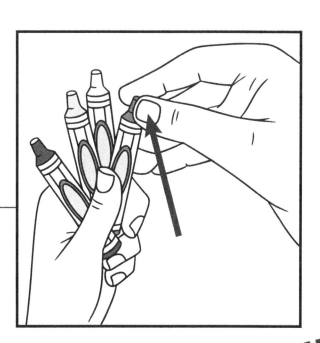

Torn Bill Trick

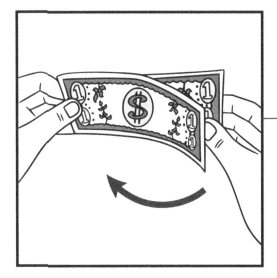

Step 1: Take one half of a dollar bill and glue it in the middle to a whole dollar bill at the top and the bottom, leaving a small pocket your finger can fit in. Let the bill dry before performing.

Step 2: Fold the corner down on the backside piece. To create the crease that will create the line to tear along.

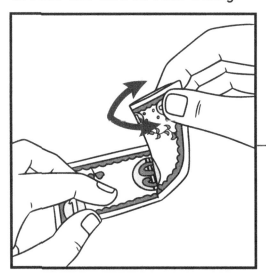

Step 3: Fold the bottom half up of the front piece.

Step 4: Fold down the top portion. Fold the bill in half, hiding the fact that there are actually three parts!

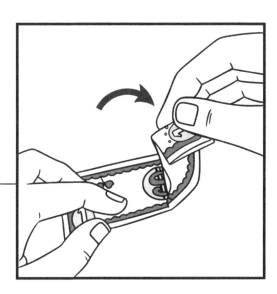

Step 5: Rip off the fake part that you glued on.

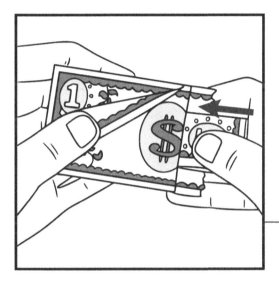

Step 6: Bring it round to the backside. Make it appear as if you are rubbing the two parts of the bill together to fix it while folding the torn piece into a small square and concealing it in the pocket you made.

Step 7: Unfold the bill.

Step 8: Make it appear as if you put it back together!

The Impassable Corks

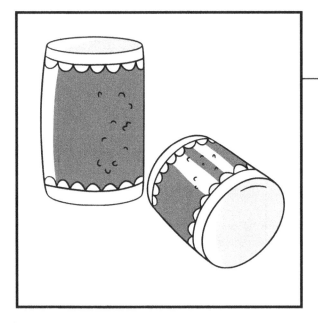

Step 1: Gather two wine corks or other cylindrical objects like tubes of chapstick to perform this trick. This trick is an optical illusion.

Step 2: Hold each cork in your palms in the pocket that your thumb and index finger make.

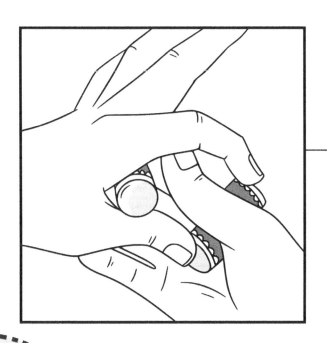

Step 3: Twist your hands so that the thumb of your right hand fits in the thumb pocket that your left hand makes.

Step 4: Your right-hand thumb will reach under the first finger of the left hand to grab the top of the cork, and

Step 5: the first finger reaches under the left thumb to grab the bottom of the cork. You may need to twist your hands fully to release both corks.

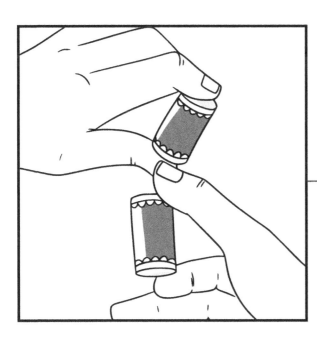

Step 6: By keeping your hands together, it will look like the corks are still intertwined. Then simply pull them apart!

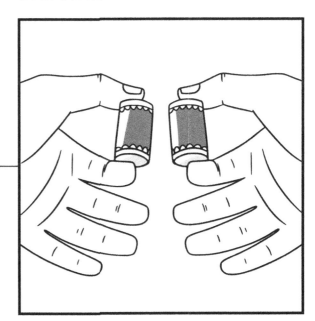

Disappearing Coin

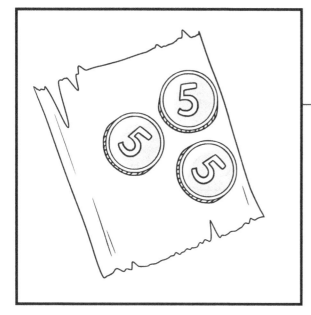

Step 1: To perform the first two disappearing coin tricks in this book, you need a small square of tinfoil and three of the same type of coins. Quarters make a great choice!

Step 2: To set up this trick, make an impression of one of the coins in the foil.

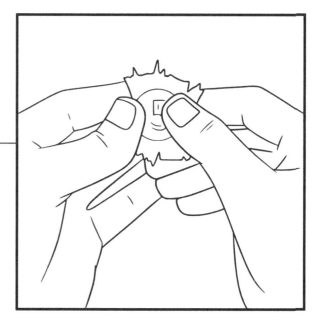

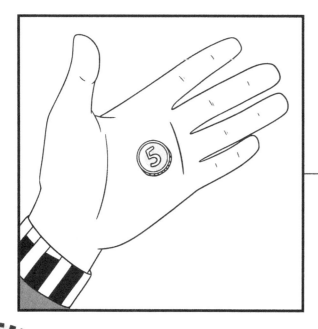

Step 3: Cut out the fake coin from the foil, making sure to leave a little extra on the sides to round off to make it look like the coin's edges.

Step 4: Place the real coins layered over the fake coin

Step 5: When you close your hand, the fake foil coin will crush, so you will only have three coins left when you open your hand!

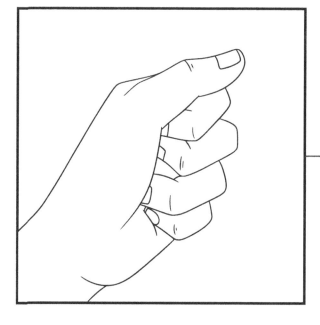

Step 6: You may need to practice with the placement of the foil coin to ensure it disappears properly when your hand is crushed.

Disappearing Coin

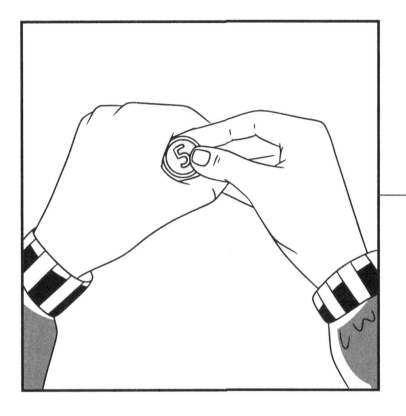

Step 1: Wear a long sleeve shirt with cuffs to easily hide your coin. Show the audience the coin to verify it's real. Make it appear as if you placed it into your palm, but keep it in the crook of your hand between your thumb and index finger.

Step 2: Keep your hand tilted up so that you can slide it onto the back of your hand.

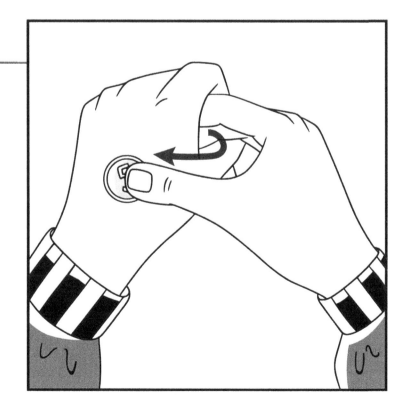

Step 3: Tilt your hand, so the coin slides down the back of your hand into your sleeve.

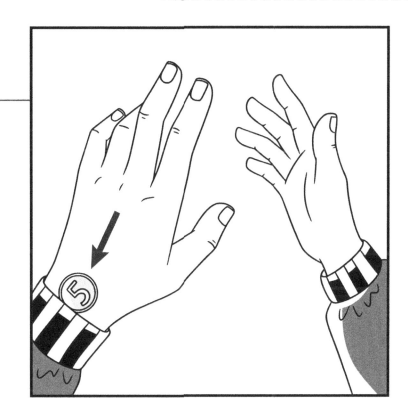

Step 4: Clap your hands together. It will appear as if the coin vanished when in reality, it slid down into your sleeve cuff.

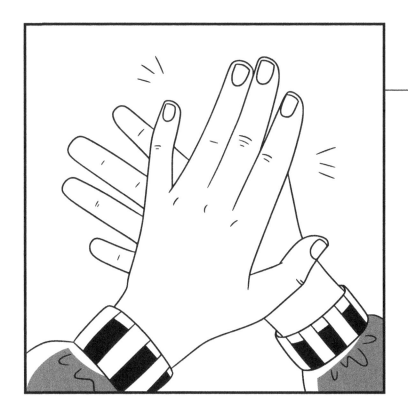

Lifting an Ice Cube With a String Trick

Step 1: Gather an ice cube, salt, a piece of string or yarn, a drinking glass, and water.

Step 2: Fill a glass with water to the brim.

Step 3: Place an ice cube on top of the water.

Step 4: Lay a piece of string over the ice cube.

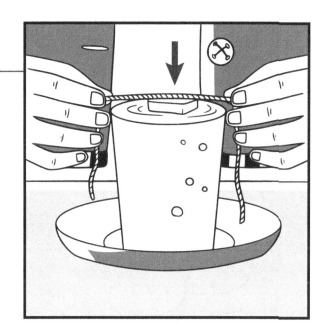

Step 5: Sprinkle some salt over the string.

Step 6: The salt will adhere the string to the ice cube, and you will be able to lift it in the air.

Egg in a Bottle

Step 1: Ask an adult for help hard boiling eggs and to use a match for this trick. Gather a wide-mouth glass bottle, hardboiled egg, match, vegetable oil, and a piece of paper.
Coat the inside of the mouth of the bottle with vegetable oil. Peel one of the hard-boiled eggs, dip it in water, and set it on the wide side on the mouth of the bottle. The egg will not fall in the bottle yet.

Step 2: Tear off a strip of paper, use a match to light it on fire, and place it quickly into the bottle.

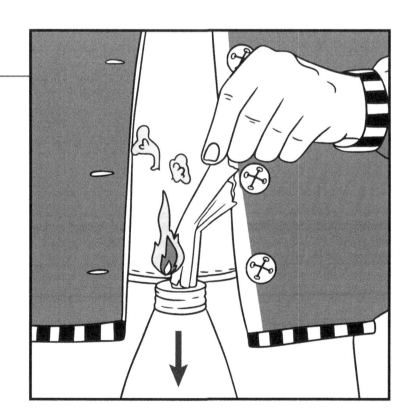

Step 5: Place the egg back on top of the bottle and watch as it now slides inside

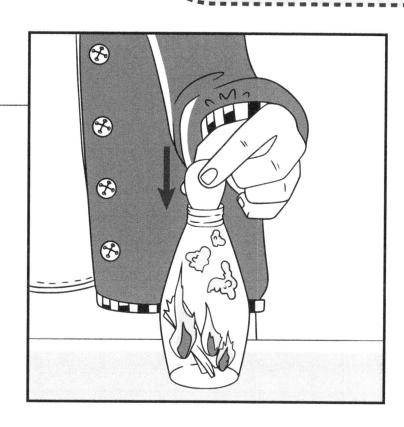

The heat from the fire makes the water molecules in the egg change and move faster, which makes the proteins of the egg begin to liquefy and become thinner.

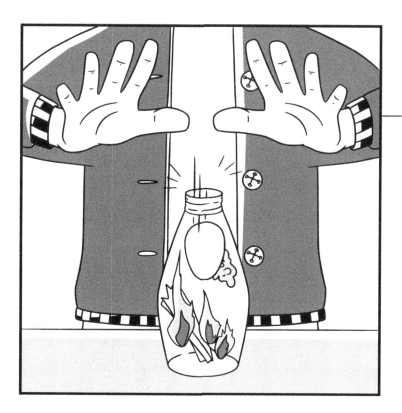

Non Bursting Balloon Trick

Step 1: Gather a balloon, a wooden skewer, and clear plastic packing tape to perform this trick.

Step 2: Blow the balloon up, tye it closed, and then put a piece of tape on each side of the balloon.

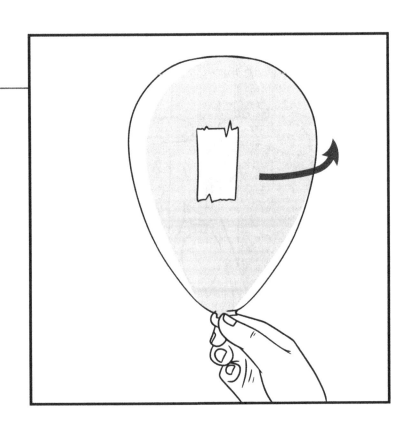

Step 3: Place the skewers through the tape on one side of the balloon and bring it out on the other side.

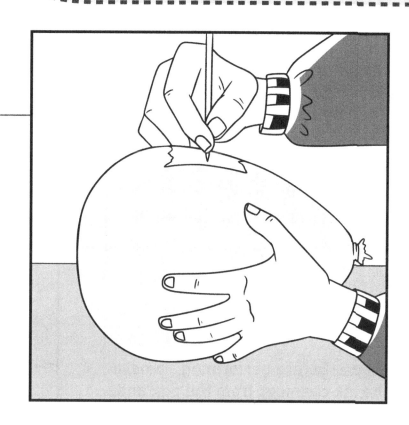

The tape creates a seal that allows you to puncture the balloon without popping it.

Floating Ring

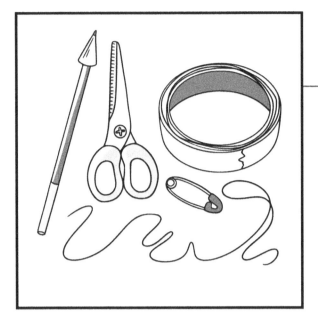

Step 1: Gather a pen where the ink chamber can be removed and replaced, invisible string, clear tape, a ring, and a safety pin.

Step 2: Before performing, remove the ink chamber from the pen and wrap the invisible string around the chamber's top.

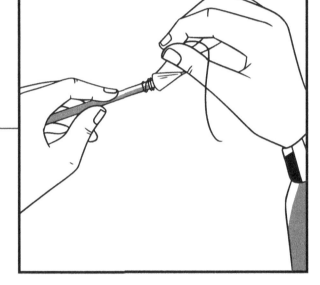

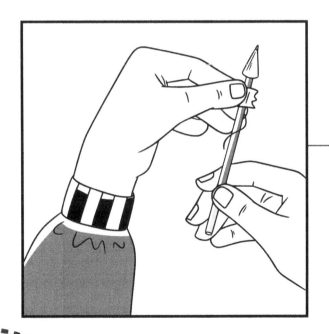

Step 3: Use some clear tape to adhere to the string.

Step 4: Once the string is secured, replace the ink chamber, and re-fasten the pen. Attach the other end of the string to the safety pin and place the pin somewhere on your clothing that is not visible to your audience.

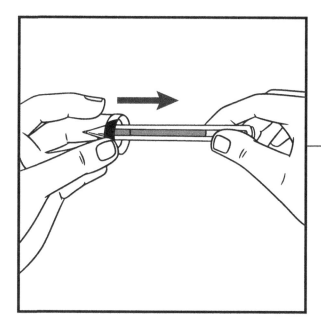

Step 5: Slide the ring over the pen. Now you are ready to amaze!

Step 6: To make it appear as if the ring is rising, move the pen away from you. The ring will look like it is rising on its own as it slides up the string. Move the pen closer to your body to lower the ring.

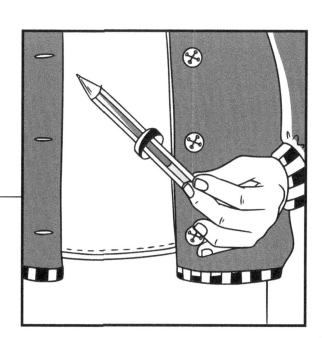

Four Aces Magic Trick

Step 1: Before performing, take all four aces from the deck and place them on the top of the deck. The audience cannot know that you've placed the aces here.

Step 2: Ask your audience participant to cut the deck into four equal piles.

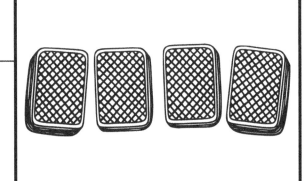

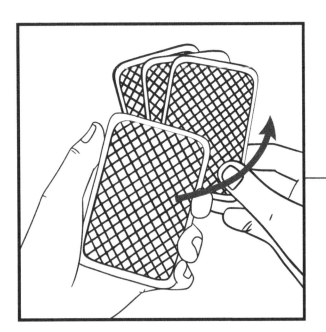

Step 3: Point to one of the three piles that do not have the aces on them, and ask your participant to take three cards off the top and place them on the bottom.

Step 4: Now ask them to take the top three cards from the pile they're holding and place one on each of the remaining piles.
Repeat this process with the other two non-ace piles.
Now your ace pile will have three random cards placed on top of the four aces.

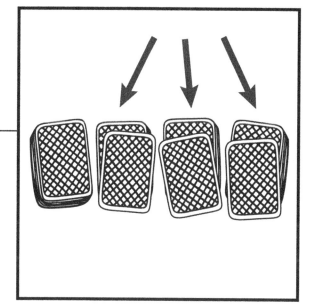

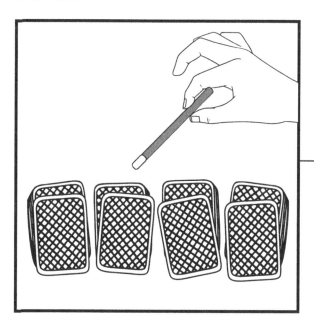

Step 5: This has set it up so that you will end up with an ace on top of each pile when they repeat the above process with the ace pile.
Perform whatever magic you'd like, a wave of the wand, magic words, etc.

Step 6: Ask your spectator to turn the top card over on each pile, revealing that you've moved the aces to the top of each pile.

Anti-Gravity Water

Step 1: Gather an empty water bottle and a piece of clear, firm plastic. Cut a circle the same size as the bottle's mouth and poke a small hole into it.

Step 2: Fill the bottle with the water.

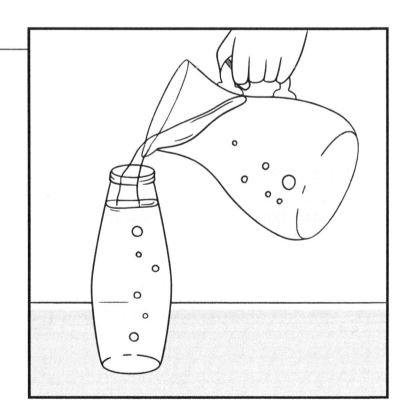

Step 4: Now ask them to take the top three cards from the pile they're holding and place one on each of the remaining piles.
Repeat this process with the other two non-ace piles.
Now your ace pile will have three random cards placed on top of the four aces.

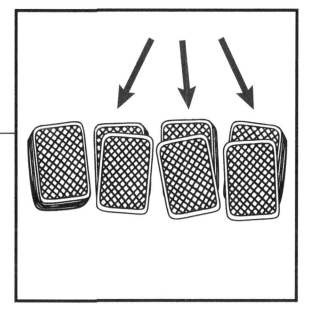

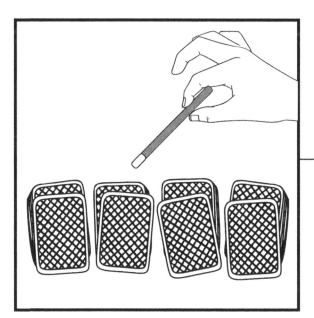

Step 5: This has set it up so that you will end up with an ace on top of each pile when they repeat the above process with the ace pile.
Perform whatever magic you'd like, a wave of the wand, magic words, etc.

Step 6: Ask your spectator to turn the top card over on each pile, revealing that you've moved the aces to the top of each pile.

Chapter 4

History of Magic

History of Magic

The root of the word magic has Greek and Latin roots from the Greek word magi. The word refers to a tribe in ancient Persia that practiced the religion Zoroastrianism.

These people believed that magicians possessed the ability to channel power through and from the deities.

People believed that the sorcerers performed spells to address the gods to ask for favors and needs.

There are also records of ancient Egyptian and Mesopotamian sorcerers.

Ancient Romans had concerns about sorcery and employed counter-sorcerers to combat evil spells and magic.

Magic was referenced in the Bible when the Three Magi or magicians visited Jesus at his birth in the stable in Bethlehem. At this point, magi were known as astronomers who could read the stars and predict things to come.

During the medieval period in Europe, magic became known as evil and developed negative connotations. People became concerned with demonic possessions, evil spirits, and elf attacks.

Specifically, the early Christian church was attacking any beliefs or customs that were connected to paganism.

At the beginning of the 11th century in Christian Europe, magic was equated to heresy and the devil's work. For the next several hundred years, Witchcraft was considered the devil's work. Burning witches at stake and drowning them became quite common. This type of magic was referred to as Black Magic.

However, during the Renaissance in Europe, there was a renewed interest in White Magic or mysticism. This was widely based on Arabic texts on alchemy and astrology.

As Europe made connections with Asian countries, the interest in magic continued. Many westerners were intrigued by the mysticism of Asian cultures.

In the mid-19th century, a deep interest in Spiritualism developed among eastern countries. Most notable among those who believed in the spirit world was First Lady Mary Todd Lincoln, wife of the 16th president of the United States Abraham Lincoln.

The Western concept of magic is supremely unique. It has combined many aspects and traits from various cultures over the decades.

In modern eras, magic or the religion of Witchcraft is still practiced by many. It is a peaceful religion connected to the natural world.

Magic has also become a major form of entertainment in modern society. In 1874, one of the most famous magicians ever known, Harry Houdini, was born. He is known as the Father of Modern Magic.

In 1902, the Society of Modern Magicians was founded, and since that time, magic as a performance art has become mainstream. 20th-century magicians such as David Copperfield and Penn & Teller have carried on early traditions of live performances.

Magic is now a well-loved performance art loved by millions worldwide and has been immortalized by books such as Harry Potter, the Magician's Trilogy, The Night Circus, and Lord of the Rings.

Whether you view magic as something natural or performance art, it has a rich and vibrant history dating back thousands of years.

Made in the USA
Middletown, DE
16 November 2021